MONTENEGRO TRAVEL GUIDE 2024 UPDATED

"All the things I wish I knew before going to Montenegro for a memorable journey through Cultural Encounters, Nature Escapes, and Urban Delights"

Harrison wells

Copyright ©2023 Harrison wells

All rights reserved.

No part of this publication may be reproduced, distributed, or transmitted in any form or by any means, including photocopying, recording, or other electronic or mechanical methods, without the prior written permission of the publisher, except in the case of brief quotations embodied in critical reviews and certain other noncommercial uses permitted by copyright law

MONTENEGRO TRAVEL GUIDE 2024 UPDATED...................................1

"All the things I wish I knew before going to Montenegro for a memorable journey through 1

WELCOME TO MONTENEGRO....6
HISTORY OF MONTENEGRO 6
KOTOR 9
WHAT TO DO 12
WHERE TO STAY 15
WHAT TO EAT 19
WHAT TO BRING HOME.................23

PODGORICA (CAPITAL) 27
WHAT TO DO....................................28
WHERE TO STAY 34
WHAT TO EAT 37
WHAT TO BRING HOME.................42

BUDVA 46
WHAT TO DO....................................46

WHERE TO STAY	49
WHAT TO EAT	52
WHAT TO BRING HOME	56

HERCEG NOVI ... 59

WHAT TO DO	61
WHERE TO STAY	64
WHAT TO EAT	67
WHAT TO BRING HOME	70

TIVAT ... 73

WHAT TO DO	75
WHERE TO STAY	79
WHAT TO EAT	81
WHAT TO BRING HOME	84

ULCINJ ... 87

WHAT TO DO	90
WHERE TO STAY	93
WHAT TO EAT	95
WHAT TO BRING HOME	99

CETINJE ... 102

WHAT TO DO 105
WHERE TO STAY 107
WHAT TO EAT 111
WHAT TO BRING HOME 115

PLAV 117

WHAT TO DO...................................119
WHERE TO STAY............................120
WHAT TO EAT 124
WHAT TO BRING HOME 126

THE BEST FOOD IN MONTENEGRO 128

FESTIVAL AND EVENT 132

NIGHTLIFE DELIGHTS...........138

10 AMAZING ITINERARIES IN MONTENEGRO 142

ADVENTUROUS EXPLORER'S DREAM (MAY - SEPTEMBER): 142
CULTURAL ENTHUSIAST'S DELIGHT (APRIL - OCTOBER):.........................143

Beach Lover's Paradise (June - September): 144
Foodie's Journey (Year-round): ..145
Historical Enthusiast's Route (April - October): 145
Nature Lover's Retreat (June - September): 146
Romantic Escape (May - September): 147
Wellness and Relaxation Retreat (Year-round): 147
Off-the-Beaten-Path Explorer (April - October): 148
Winter Wonderland (December - March): 149

TRAVELLING PRACTICALITIES 149

CONCLUSION 155

WELCOME TO MONTENEGRO

Welcome to Montenegro, a hidden gem nestled in the heart of the Balkans, where history and natural beauty converge in spectacular fashion. Did you know that Montenegro's coastline, spanning a mere 293 kilometers, encompasses some of the most breathtaking fjords in Europe? This includes the awe-inspiring Bay of Kotor, a UNESCO World Heritage site, often likened to a submerged river canyon.

HISTORY OF MONTENEGRO

Montenegro, ensconced within the formidable terrain of the Balkan Peninsula, stands as a living testament to the ebb and flow of history, mirroring the ruggedness of its landscape. Its origins are rooted in antiquity, with evidence of human presence dating back to the Bronze Age. This land, strategically positioned along ancient trade routes, became a crossroads of cultures, attracting the likes of the Illyrians, Greeks, and Romans.

In 9 AD, Montenegro was incorporated into the Roman province of Dalmatia, initiating an era of Romanization that bequeathed to posterity impressive archaeological vestiges. With the waning of the Roman Empire, Montenegro witnessed a succession of dominions by various barbarian tribes—the Goths, Huns, and Byzantines—before finding integration into the medieval Slavic state of Duklja in the 9th century.

Duklja metamorphosed into the Principality of Zeta, characterized by a synthesis of Slavic and Byzantine influences. The 14th century proved pivotal, as the ascendancy of the House of Balšić ushered in an epoch of cultural efflorescence and prosperous trade. Nevertheless, the region's strategic allure made it a coveted prize for competing powers, with the Venetian Republic among those vying for dominion.

The 15th century bore witness to the inexorable advance of the Ottoman Empire through the Balkans, etching an indelible imprint on Montenegro's narrative. In response, a resolute spirit of resistance surged forth, culminating in the establishment of the independent Principality of Montenegro under the aegis of the Petrović-Njegoš dynasty. Over the centuries, Montenegro defied Ottoman incursions, crystallizing its identity as a symbol of defiance against imperial dominance.

The 19th century unfolded as a chapter of Montenegro's quest for international recognition. Under the stewardship of Petar II Petrović-Njegoš, the Principality secured acknowledgment at the Congress of Berlin in 1878, cementing its status as an autonomous entity. The ensuing reign of Nicholas I witnessed a rapid metamorphosis, with fervent efforts to forge a centralized state and foster infrastructural growth.

The early 20th century introduced seismic shifts as Montenegro grappled with the intricate geopolitics of the Balkans. In 1918, it forged a union with Serbia, giving rise to the Kingdom of Serbs, Croats, and Slovenes, a precursor to Yugoslavia. Montenegro weathered turbulent decades marked by political upheaval, monarchy, and the ascent of communism.

The disintegration of Yugoslavia in the 1990s propelled Montenegro onto a path toward independence. A decisive referendum in 2006 firmly established its status as a sovereign nation. Since then, Montenegro has steadfastly worked towards stability and economic advancement, positioning itself as a candidate for accession to the European Union.

Today, Montenegro proudly stands as a living testament to its storied past. Its cultural heritage, steeped in diversity, echoes through its stunning landscapes, and its people embody a spirit of resilience that has endured through the ages. From the ancient Illyrians to the defiance against empires, Montenegro's history is a mirror to the indomitable spirit of its inhabitants and their unwavering pursuit of self-determination.

Kotor

Ancient Origins (c. 168 BC - 476 AD): The roots of Kotor trace back to ancient times when it was known as Acruvium, founded by the ancient Romans around 168 BC. As a strategic outpost along the Adriatic coast, it played a crucial role in maritime trade and military defense. Over the centuries, Kotor came under the influence of various empires, including the Byzantines and the Venetians, leaving an indelible mark on its culture and architecture.

Medieval Ascendancy (476 AD - 1499): With the fall of the Western Roman Empire in the 5th century, Kotor found itself under the rule of the Byzantine Empire, which maintained control for several centuries. However, the city's strategic location made it a coveted prize, leading to numerous conflicts. In 1420, Kotor was annexed by the Venetian Republic, marking the beginning of a new era. The Venetians fortified the city, constructing the formidable walls and the iconic Kotor Fortress that still stands today.

Ottoman Interlude (1499 - 1684): In 1499, following a brief period of Venetian control, Kotor fell under Ottoman rule. This period brought about cultural and architectural influences from the Ottoman Empire, leaving a lasting impact on the town's character. However, tensions persisted, and Kotor witnessed a series of battles and shifting allegiances over the ensuing decades.

Habsburg Rule and Napoleon's Conquest (1684 - 1814): After a prolonged period of conflict, the Habsburg Monarchy captured Kotor in 1684, marking a significant shift in power dynamics. Under Habsburg rule, Kotor flourished economically and culturally. However, the Napoleonic Wars saw the French Empire take control of the region in 1807. The city was renamed "Cattaro" during this period.

Austro-Hungarian Era and Yugoslav Yugoslavia (1814 - 1991): The Congress of Vienna in 1814 returned Kotor to Austrian rule. It remained a part of the Austro-Hungarian Empire until its dissolution in 1918. Following World War I, Kotor became part of the newly-formed Kingdom of Serbs, Croats, and Slovenes, later known as Yugoslavia. Through the turbulent 20th century, the town endured political changes, including the socialist era under Josip Broz Tito.

Contemporary Kotor (1991 - Present): With the disintegration of Yugoslavia in the early 1990s,

Montenegro declared independence from Serbia in 2006, solidifying its status as an independent nation. Kotor, with its UNESCO-listed Old Town and breathtaking bay, emerged as a thriving tourist destination, attracting visitors from around the world. Today, it stands as a living testament to its rich history, where ancient fortifications stand alongside vibrant cafes, preserving the legacy of a town that has endured and prospered for over two millennia.

Kotor's history, marked by a tapestry of empires and cultures, continues to shape its character, making it a captivating destination for those seeking to explore the echoes of time in this Adriatic jewel.

WHAT TO DO

Historical Enthusiasts: Kotor Old Town

Uniqueness: Kotor Old Town is a living time capsule, a UNESCO World Heritage Site that has preserved its medieval architecture in remarkable detail. Stepping into its narrow, winding streets is like entering a different era. The town boasts an array of churches and cathedrals, each with its own architectural story to tell. The towering walls that encircle the town have stood sentinel for centuries, protecting its rich history.

Directions: Kotor Old Town is conveniently nestled right along the waterfront. If you're driving, you'll find parking lots just outside the city walls. For those arriving from other parts of Montenegro, buses and taxis are readily available and will bring you directly to the Old Town's entrance.

Nature Lovers: Kotor Bay and Lovćen National Park

Uniqueness: The Bay of Kotor, affectionately referred to as Europe's southernmost fjord, is a natural masterpiece. Towering mountains rise dramatically from the water, creating a spectacular panorama. The bay's calm, deep-blue waters provide a serene contrast to the rugged terrain. Lovćen National Park, within proximity, offers a different facet of natural beauty with its crisscrossing hiking trails and staggering vistas of the bay.

Year Founded: While the bay's geological formation is ancient, Lovćen National Park was formally established in 1952, preserving the area's diverse flora and fauna.

Directions: Kotor Bay is easily accessible from Kotor itself. If you're driving, follow the shoreline road for a continuous view of the bay. Lovćen

National Park is a short drive (approximately 30 minutes) from Kotor, with well-marked roads guiding you through the scenic route leading to the park.

Art and Culture Aficionados: Maritime Museum

Uniqueness: Housed within an exquisite Baroque palace, the Maritime Museum of Montenegro invites visitors to embark on a maritime journey through the Adriatic's history. The museum's collection of artifacts, including intricate model ships, ancient navigational instruments, and maritime documents, offers a vivid portrayal of the region's seafaring heritage.

Year Founded: The Maritime Museum was established in 1900, a tribute to the enduring maritime traditions that have shaped the region.

Directions: Conveniently situated within the Old Town of Kotor, the Maritime Museum is easily accessible on foot. Its central location makes it a captivating stop for visitors exploring the historic heart of the town.

Adventure Seekers: Hiking the City Walls

Uniqueness: Embarking on a hike up the city walls of Kotor offers an unparalleled perspective of this historic town and its awe-inspiring surroundings. The walls ascend the mountainside in a zigzag pattern, creating not only a challenging trek but also a platform for panoramic views of Kotor Bay. This elevated vantage point imparts an understanding of the town's strategic positioning and the natural beauty that embraces it.

Year Founded: The initial walls trace back to the 9th century, with significant expansions occurring during the Venetian era to fortify the town against potential adversaries.

Directions: The trailhead for the city walls hike is conveniently situated within the Old Town of Kotor. Clear signage will guide you from the town's central square toward the beginning of the path. The ascent may be steep, so comfortable footwear is recommended for this adventure.

WHERE TO STAY

For History Enthusiasts: Hotel Astoria

Unique Beauty: Nestled within the ancient walls of Kotor's Old Town, **Hotel Astoria** is a true gem for history enthusiasts. The moment you step inside, you're transported to a bygone era. The architecture is a harmonious blend of old-world charm and modern comfort. The stone walls exude a sense of timelessness, while the wooden beams and period décor add an authentic touch. Every corner of the hotel is steeped in history, creating an immersive experience for guests.

Local Perspective: Among locals, **Hotel Astoria** holds a special place for its unwavering commitment to preserving the heritage of the Old Town. The painstaking effort to maintain the authenticity of the building is highly appreciated. The staff, known for their warmth and attentiveness, further enhance the experience. They often go above and beyond to ensure guests have a memorable stay, leaving a lasting impression on visitors.

For Nature Lovers: Hotel Forza Mare

Unique Beauty: Hotel Forza Mare is a sanctuary for nature lovers, perched along the tranquil shores of Kotor Bay. The beauty of this hotel lies not only in its stunning views of the bay and the majestic surrounding mountains but also in its commitment to eco-friendliness. The serene garden provides a peaceful retreat, and the private beach area offers a direct connection to the azure waters of the bay. The rooms are meticulously designed to harmonize with the natural surroundings, creating a seamless blend of comfort and environmental consciousness.

Local Perspective: Both locals and visitors alike sing praises for Hotel Forza Mare. It's often regarded as a haven for those seeking a respite from the hustle and bustle of daily life. The idyllic location by the bay is particularly cherished, providing a perfect setting for relaxation and rejuvenation. Many locals recommend this hotel as the ultimate destination for a tranquil retreat by the water's edge.

For Art and Culture Aficionados: Boutique Hotel Hippocampus

Unique Beauty: Boutique Hotel Hippocampus stands as a testament to the artistry and cultural richness of Kotor. Housed in a meticulously restored historic building within the heart of the Old Town, this boutique hotel offers a striking fusion of contemporary aesthetics and local heritage. The design pays homage to the town's cultural legacy, seamlessly blending modern elements with traditional motifs. The result is an atmosphere of refined elegance that celebrates the artistic spirit of Kotor.

Local Perspective: This hotel receives high praise from both locals and travelers for its exceptional attention to detail in showcasing Kotor's cultural tapestry. The curated art displays and cultural events hosted within the hotel are often lauded for their contribution to the local artistic community. The efforts put forth to preserve and celebrate Kotor's rich cultural heritage resonate deeply with those who hold the town's legacy close to their hearts.

For Adventure Seekers: Hotel Palazzo Radomiri

Unique Beauty: Hotel Palazzo Radomiri is a testament to both history and adventure, perfectly situated on the waterfront of Kotor Bay. This meticulously restored 18th-century stone villa exudes an aura of timeless charm. It seamlessly marries traditional architectural elements with modern amenities, creating a haven for explorers. The private jetty adds an exciting dimension, offering easy access to water-based activities and adventures on the bay.

Local Perspective: Locals hold Hotel Palazzo Radomiri in high regard for its picturesque location and steadfast commitment to preserving the historic essence of the building. The hotel stands as a beacon, inviting travelers to immerse themselves in the natural wonders and cultural richness of the bay and its surroundings. It's often recommended as an ideal base for those looking to embark on waterborne adventures or simply soak in the breathtaking vistas.

For Foodies: Hotel Casa del Mare - Amfora

Unique Beauty: Hotel Casa del Mare - Amfora is a culinary haven, located in the picturesque Dobrota area just a short drive from Kotor. The hotel's contemporary and elegant design is perfectly complemented by panoramic views of the bay. Every aspect of the hotel is carefully curated to create an atmosphere of refinement and serenity. The real highlight, however, is the restaurant. Here, the chefs skillfully craft delectable Mediterranean cuisine that celebrates the abundance of fresh, local ingredients.

Local Perspective: Both locals and visitors alike hold Hotel Casa del Mare - Amfora in high esteem for its exquisite dining experience and the serene ambiance it provides. The restaurant's dedication to showcasing the flavors of the region, coupled with the tranquil setting overlooking the bay, creates a truly immersive culinary journey. This hotel is often recommended for those who seek not only a comfortable stay but also an opportunity to savor the authentic tastes of the local cuisine in a peaceful and elegant setting.

WHAT TO EAT

For Seafood Enthusiasts:

Restaurant: *Konoba Scala Santa*

Must-Eat: The Grilled Adriatic Fish Platter at Konoba Scala Santa is a seafood lover's dream. It typically features a selection of locally caught fish, seasoned and grilled to perfection. Expect a medley of flavors that capture the essence of the Adriatic Sea.

Must-Drink: Pairing the fish platter with a local Montenegrin white wine enhances the dining experience. The crisp, fruity notes of the white wine complement the delicate flavors of the seafood.

Address: Stari Grad 427, 85330 Kotor, Montenegro.

Directions: To find Konoba Scala Santa, start at the main gate (Sea Gate) of Kotor's Old Town. Head straight into the narrow cobblestone streets and take a left at the Clock Tower. As you continue, keep an eye out on your right side for the charming facade of the restaurant.

For History Buffs:

Restaurant: Galion

Must-Eat: Galion is known for its Boka Bay Seafood Risotto. This dish embodies the rich maritime history of Kotor, combining locally sourced seafood with Arborio rice and a blend of flavorful herbs and spices.

Must-Drink: Immerse yourself in the local culture by trying the Homemade Pomegranate Rakija. This traditional Montenegrin brandy offers a unique taste and a touch of authenticity to your dining experience.

Address: Stari grad 422, 85330 Kotor, Montenegro.

Directions: As you enter the Old Town through the Sea Gate, turn right and stroll along the picturesque waterfront. Galion is located near the end of the promenade, offering stunning views of the bay.

For Vegetarians and Vegans:

Restaurant: Tanjga

Must-Eat: Tanjga caters to vegetarians and vegans with its flavorful Vegan Buddha Bowl. This dish typically includes a colorful assortment of fresh vegetables, grains, and plant-based protein sources, all topped with a delicious dressing.

Must-Drink: Opt for a refreshing Freshly Squeezed Fruit Juice to complement the vibrant flavors of the Buddha Bowl and to stay hydrated.

Address: Škurda 413, 85330 Kotor, Montenegro.

Directions: Tanjga is situated outside the city walls, near the northern entrance to the Old Town. After exiting through the River Gate, follow the road to the right. You'll spot Tanjga on your left.

For Adventurous Palates:

Restaurant: Bastion

Must-Eat: For those seeking unique and bold flavors, the Black Risotto with Cuttlefish Ink at Bastion is a must-try. This dish showcases the culinary creativity of the region, offering a combination of rich, briny seafood with the distinctive taste of cuttlefish ink.

Must-Drink: Explore the local craft beer selection to find the perfect accompaniment to your adventurous meal.

Address: Stari grad 313, 85330 Kotor, Montenegro.

Directions: Bastion is nestled within the winding streets of the Old Town. Upon entering through the Sea Gate, take a left turn at the Clock Tower and follow the signs guiding you to Bastion.

For Romantic Evenings:

Restaurant: Cesarica

Must-Eat: Elevate your romantic evening with the Lobster with Truffle Sauce at Cesarica. This luxurious dish combines the delicate sweetness of lobster with the earthy aroma of truffles, creating a truly indulgent experience.

Must-Drink: Pair your meal with a fine Montenegrin Red Wine, enhancing the flavors and setting the mood for a memorable evening.

Address: Trg od Brasna, Stari grad, 85330 Kotor, Montenegro.

Directions: To find Cesarica, enter the Old Town through the Sea Gate and walk straight. When you reach the square with the Cathedral of Saint Tryphon, turn left. Cesarica is located on the charming square just behind the cathedral.

WHAT TO BRING HOME

For Art Enthusiasts:

Gift/Souvenir: Hand-Painted Ceramics

Where to Get Them: The "Clay Gallery" in Kotor is a treasure trove for art enthusiasts. Here, you'll find a stunning collection of hand-painted ceramics, each piece reflecting the artistic talent and cultural richness of the region.

Address: Clay Gallery Kotor, Trg od Salate, 85330 Kotor, Montenegro.

Directions: Starting at the main gate (Sea Gate) of Kotor's Old Town, walk straight ahead and take a left turn at the Clock Tower. As you continue along this charming street, keep an eye out for the Clay Gallery on your right. Its distinctive facade adorned with ceramics is hard to miss.

For Foodies:

Gift/Souvenir: Local Olive Oil and Honey Products

Where to Get Them: The "Marketplace of Kotor" (Pijaca od Kotor) is a bustling market where foodies can explore and sample an array of locally-produced olive oil and honey products. The market is a sensory delight, offering a taste of the region's culinary heritage.

Address: Pijaca od Kotor, Stari grad, 85330 Kotor, Montenegro.

Directions: After entering the Old Town through the Sea Gate, turn left and follow the cobblestone streets. You'll soon arrive at the lively marketplace, where vendors display their bounty of olive oil and honey products, often with samples available for tasting.

For History Buffs:

Gift/Souvenir: Antique Maps and Nautical Charts

Where to Get Them: The "Antique Shop" near the Maritime Museum is a haven for history buffs. Here, you'll discover a curated selection of antique maps and nautical charts that offer a glimpse into the maritime legacy of Kotor.

Address: Antique Shop, 8 Stari Grad, Kotor, Montenegro.

Directions: As you step through the Sea Gate into the Old Town, continue straight ahead. Once you reach the Maritime Museum, you'll find the Antique Shop nearby. Its facade, adorned with maritime memorabilia, makes it easily identifiable.

For Fashion and Jewelry Lovers:

Gift/Souvenir: Handmade Silver Jewelry

Where to Get Them: "Silver Hand" is a boutique jewelry store that caters to fashion and jewelry enthusiasts. The shop showcases a stunning array of handcrafted silver jewelry pieces, each a testament to the skill and craftsmanship of local artisans.

Address: Silver Hand, Stari grad 476, 85330 Kotor, Montenegro.

Directions: Starting from the main gate (Sea Gate), walk straight and take a left at the Clock Tower. Continue along the street, and you'll spot Silver Hand on your left. Its elegant storefront and intricate jewelry displays invite you to step inside.

For Nature Enthusiasts:

Gift/Souvenir: Lavender Products

Where to Get Them: "Mala Radnja Lavande" (Little Lavender Shop) is a charming store that caters to nature enthusiasts. It offers a delightful range of lavender-based products, from fragrant sachets to essential oils, providing a touch of nature's tranquility.

Address: Mala Radnja Lavande, Stari grad 284, 85330 Kotor, Montenegro.

Directions: Upon entering the Old Town through the Sea Gate, walk straight ahead and take the first right turn. Mala Radnja Lavande awaits on your left, with its inviting displays of lavender products.

PODGORICA (CAPITAL)

Podgorica, often referred to as the "City of Wells" due to its numerous natural springs, has a rich history dating back over two millennia. It's one of Europe's oldest continuously inhabited cities, with evidence of settlements as far back as the Roman era. Additionally, Podgorica holds the distinction of being one of the few European capitals without a medieval old town, owing to its turbulent past.

Podgorica's history is a chronicle of conquests, with influences from the Roman, Byzantine, Ottoman, and Austro-Hungarian empires. It's a city that has risen from the ashes, having been nearly leveled during World War II and rebuilt in the modernist style under socialist rule. This history is etched into the cityscape, where remnants of old fortifications stand side by side with contemporary architecture, offering a unique blend of the ancient and the modern.

While Podgorica may not boast a well-preserved medieval old town, it harbors its own treasures waiting to be discovered. The Millennium Bridge, an architectural marvel, spans the Moraca River, offering breathtaking views of the city. The historic Clock Tower and the Montenegrin National Theater are testaments to the city's cultural heritage. As you explore the city's parks and squares, you'll encounter sculptures and monuments that tell stories of Montenegro's struggles and triumphs.

Life in Podgorica pulsates with a vibrant energy. The city is a melting pot of cultures, where locals and visitors alike gather in lively cafes, bustling markets, and verdant parks. The Montenegrin spirit of hospitality is evident in the warm smiles and welcoming gestures of its people. The culinary scene is a testament to the city's diverse influences, with offerings ranging from traditional Montenegrin dishes to international flavors.

WHAT TO DO

For History Enthusiasts:

Visit the Petrovic Palace (Dvorac Petrovića)

Uniqueness:

The Petrovic Palace, an architectural gem nestled in the heart of Podgorica, stands as a living testament to Montenegro's royal legacy. Once the residence of the Petrovic ruling family, this historic palace exudes an air of regal elegance. Its architecture is a captivating blend of styles, bearing witness to the diverse influences that have shaped Montenegro's history over the centuries. From the graceful lines of Venetian design to the grandeur of Ottoman motifs, the palace is a chronicle of epochs past.

Year Founded:

This majestic residence first graced the Podgorica skyline in the 18th century, a time when Montenegro's cultural tapestry was being woven with threads of history and tradition.

Directions:

To immerse yourself in this rich historical experience, head southeast from the city center towards the venerable Njegoševa Street. Follow the path, letting the city's essence guide you, and soon you'll stand before the Petrovic Palace, its grandeur poised to transport you back in time.

For Nature Lovers:

Stroll along Gorica Hill and Millennium Bridge

Uniqueness:

Gorica Hill, a verdant haven amidst the urban sprawl of Podgorica, beckons nature enthusiasts with its panoramic views. Here, the city's hustle and bustle fade into the background, replaced by a sense of serenity and natural splendor. The Millennium Bridge, a triumph of modern engineering, serves as a gateway, seamlessly connecting Gorica Hill to the city center. Its graceful arches stretch across the Moraca River, a testament to human ingenuity.

Year Founded:

In the 21st century, a new chapter in Podgorica's story began with the development of Gorica Hill and the construction of the Millennium Bridge, an emblem of progress and connectivity. The bridge officially opened its gates to the world in 2005.

Directions:

Embark on your journey from Republic Square, the heart of the city. Head southeast along Hercegovacka Street, letting the anticipation of natural beauty guide your steps. As you continue, the base of Gorica Hill will welcome you, inviting you to ascend to its tranquil heights and cross the Millennium Bridge.

For Art and Culture Aficionados:

Explore the Contemporary Art Center of Montenegro (Centar Savremene Umjetnosti Crne Gore)

Uniqueness:

Within the walls of the Contemporary Art Center of Montenegro, a vibrant tapestry of artistic expression unfolds. This center stands as a beacon for contemporary art, a space where creativity knows no bounds. It hosts a kaleidoscope of exhibitions, performances, and cultural events, showcasing the diverse visions of both local and international artists. Here, the avant-garde mingles with tradition, offering a window into the dynamic world of modern Montenegrin artistry.

Year Founded:

In the year 1991, this cultural hub emerged, its doors opening wide to welcome the artistic community and enthusiasts alike.

Directions:

Embark on a southward journey from Republic Square along the inviting Hercegovacka Street. Let the rhythm of the city guide you, and soon, on the right side, you'll encounter the Contemporary Art Center, nestled near the Cultural and Information

Center **_'Budo Tomović'_**. Here, the vibrant pulse of creativity beckons you to step inside and explore the boundless realms of contemporary art.

For Outdoor Enthusiasts:

Visit Skadar Lake National Park (Nacionalni park Skadarsko jezero)

Uniqueness:

In the heart of Montenegro lies a natural treasure, Skadar Lake, the largest lake in the Balkan Peninsula. Its shores cradle a haven of biodiversity, where avian symphonies fill the air, and the dance of flora and fauna unfolds in harmonious rhythm. For birdwatchers, nature lovers, and those seeking outdoor adventure, this paradise offers an unrivaled sanctuary. Kayaking through pristine waters or hiking along rugged trails, every step is a communion with the untamed beauty of nature.

Year Founded:

The year 1983 marked the official establishment of Skadar Lake National Park, a testament to Montenegro's dedication to preserving its ecological treasures.

Directions:

Embark on a scenic journey by taking the M-2.3 highway southward from Podgorica. The road will lead you through picturesque landscapes, and in approximately 30 minutes, you'll arrive at the enchanting shores of Skadar Lake. Here, nature's symphony awaits, inviting you to become part of its intricate tapestry.

For Shopping and Local Cuisine Enthusiasts:

Explore the City Mall and Try Local Restaurants

Uniqueness:

In the heart of Podgorica, City Mall stands as a beacon for shoppers, a sprawling emporium where a world of choices unfolds. It's the largest shopping center in the city, offering an eclectic array of shops, cafes, and entertainment options. After indulging in retail therapy, embark on a culinary adventure, savoring the rich tapestry of Montenegrin cuisine at nearby restaurants. From hearty traditional dishes to international flavors, every bite is a celebration of local flavors.

Year Founded:

The year 2013 heralded the opening of City Mall, a modern oasis for those seeking retail therapy and gastronomic delights.

Directions:

Set your course from Republic Square, and venture southeast along Hercegovacka Street. The path will lead you directly to City Mall, its vibrant façade beckoning you to explore the myriad offerings within. After a satisfying shopping spree, nearby restaurants await, ready to serve you a taste of Montenegro's rich culinary heritage.

WHERE TO STAY

Hotel Hilton Podgorica Crna Gora

Unique Beauty:

The Hilton Podgorica Crna Gora is a testament to refined luxury that seamlessly blends with Montenegrin elegance. The hotel boasts a contemporary design with clean lines and opulent accents, creating an atmosphere of modern sophistication. However, what truly sets it apart is its prime location along the picturesque Moraca River. The views of the flowing waters, coupled with the surrounding lush greenery, offer a serene backdrop to the urban oasis that is the Hilton. This fusion of natural beauty and contemporary design makes it a standout choice for discerning travelers seeking both luxury and authenticity in Podgorica.

Hotel New Star

Unique Beauty:

A jewel in Podgorica's hospitality scene, Hotel New Star is celebrated for its sleek and minimalist design. Every facet of this boutique hotel exudes a sense of understated elegance, from the clean lines of its architecture to the refined simplicity of its interiors. What truly sets it apart, however, is its rooftop terrace. Here, guests are treated to panoramic views that stretch across the city, offering a breathtaking vantage point from which to take in the dynamic skyline of Podgorica. This elevated retreat becomes an ideal spot to unwind, creating an experience that is as unique as it is unforgettable.

Hotel Podgorica

Unique Beauty:

Hotel Podgorica weaves together the threads of history and modernity, creating a tapestry of charm that reflects the city's heritage. With roots dating back to the 1960s, this establishment exudes a mid-century modern aesthetic. The design elements pay homage to a bygone era while seamlessly integrating Montenegrin hospitality. The heart of the city beats just outside its doors, allowing guests to easily access the various attractions and experiences that Podgorica has to offer. This combination of timeless design and central location provides a distinct ambiance that is both welcoming and evocative.

Hotel Hemera

Unique Beauty:

Hotel Hemera stands as a testament to contemporary design principles, creating an atmosphere that is both sleek and inviting. Natural materials are artfully incorporated, infusing the space with a sense of warmth and tranquility. From the moment guests step into the lobby, they are enveloped in an ambiance that fosters relaxation and rejuvenation. The focus on comfort permeates every aspect of the hotel, from the thoughtfully designed rooms to the inviting common areas. This emphasis on creating a calming atmosphere sets Hotel Hemera apart, offering guests a sanctuary in the heart of Podgorica.

Hotel Evropa

Unique Beauty:

Stepping into Hotel Evropa is akin to taking a journey back in time. As one of the oldest hotels in Podgorica, it exudes a historic charm that is palpable from the moment you enter. The elegant architecture and classic interior design elements transport guests to a bygone era, where time seems to slow down. The hotel's corridors echo with the whispers of history, while the carefully preserved details harken back to a more gracious age. Staying at Hotel Evropa is a true immersion into the heritage of Podgorica, offering a unique experience that blends the past with the present in a seamless tapestry of beauty and hospitality.

WHAT TO EAT

For Authentic Montenegrin Cuisine:

Restaurant: Pod Volat

Must-Eat: At Pod Volat, the Njeguški Steak is a culinary masterpiece. This dish perfectly encapsulates the essence of Montenegrin cuisine, featuring a tender grilled steak adorned with locally sourced Njeguši cheese and savory prosciutto. The blend of flavors creates a symphony on the palate, offering a taste of tradition and regional excellence.

Must-Drink: Pairing this delectable dish with a Montenegrin Vranac Red Wine is nothing short of an enchanting experience. The robust notes of this indigenous red wine harmonize with the flavors of the steak, enhancing every bite with a rich and velvety texture.

Directions: To reach Pod Volat, navigate towards 18 Vaka Đurovića, Podgorica 81000. Starting from the city center, head northwest on Bulevar Svetog Petra Cetinjskog, then make a left onto Vaka Đurovića. You'll find the restaurant on the left, ready to offer an unforgettable taste of Montenegro.

For Seafood Lovers:

Restaurant: Konoba Mostina

Must-Eat: Konoba Mostina invites seafood enthusiasts to savor the Grilled Adriatic Sea Bass, a masterpiece of maritime delight. This dish showcases the freshest catch, seasoned with a delicate blend of local herbs and expertly grilled to perfection. Each bite is a voyage along the coast, offering a taste of the Adriatic's bounty.

Must-Drink: To complement the flavors of the sea bass, a glass of Krstač White Wine is the perfect choice. Its crisp and aromatic profile elevates the dining experience, creating a harmonious balance with the seafood's natural essence.

Directions: Journey to 38 Vasa Raičkovića, Podgorica 81000 to discover Konoba Mostina. Departing from the city center, head southeast on Njegoševa, then take a right onto Vasa Raičkovića. The restaurant awaits on your right, promising a memorable seafood adventure.

For Vegetarian and Vegan Options:

Restaurant: Gulaš Restoran

Must-Eat: Gulaš Restoran caters to vegetarians and vegans with their delectable Vegan Goulash. This hearty stew combines an array of vibrant vegetables, stewed to perfection with a medley of savory spices. Each spoonful is a celebration of plant-based goodness, offering a comforting and flavorful dining experience.

Must-Drink: Complementing this wholesome dish, a glass of Freshly Squeezed Pomegranate Juice offers a refreshing burst of natural vitality. Its invigorating flavors provide the perfect accompaniment to the nourishing vegan goulash.

Directions: Navigate to 11 Novaka Miloševa, Podgorica 81000 to indulge in Gulaš Restoran's delectable offerings. Departing from the city center, travel south on Slobode, then make a right onto Novaka Miloševa. The restaurant awaits on your right, ready to treat you to a delightful plant-based culinary experience.

For International Cuisine:

Restaurant: Plato

Must-Eat: At Plato, the Chicken Alfredo Pasta takes center stage. This dish is a culinary symphony, featuring tender pieces of chicken enveloped in a creamy Alfredo sauce, served over perfectly cooked fettuccine pasta. Every forkful is a medley of flavors and textures, offering a taste of international indulgence right in the heart of Podgorica.

Must-Drink: The Espresso Martini at Plato is a delightful concoction that serves as the perfect conclusion to a satisfying meal. This cocktail, blending the boldness of coffee with the smoothness of vodka, provides a delightful kick of caffeine-infused decadence.

Directions: To discover the culinary delights of Plato, venture to 7 Novaka Miloševa, Podgorica 81000. Departing from the city center, travel south on Slobode, then make a right onto Novaka

Miloševa. The restaurant welcomes you on your left, offering a global gastronomic experience.

For Fine Dining Experience:

Restaurant: Murano

Must-Eat: Murano offers a culinary masterpiece with its Beef Tenderloin with Truffle Sauce. This dish is an embodiment of culinary artistry, featuring succulent beef tenderloin paired with a decadent truffle-infused sauce. The marriage of flavors and textures creates an unforgettable dining experience that elevates fine dining to new heights.

Must-Drink: Complementing this exquisite dish, a glass of Montenegrin Cabernet Sauvignon is the ideal choice. This bold red wine, with its well-balanced character, harmonizes seamlessly with the richness of the beef tenderloin, creating a symphony of taste sensations.

Directions: To experience the epitome of fine dining, make your way to 34a Njegoševa, Podgorica 81000. Starting from the city center, head northwest on Bulevar Svetog Petra Cetinjskog, then turn left onto Njegoševa. The restaurant awaits on your right, ready to offer an exceptional fine dining experience in Podgorica.

WHAT TO BRING HOME

For Art Enthusiasts:

Gift/Souvenir: Montenegrin Handicrafts and Paintings

Where to Get Them: Art Market "Kolekcija"

Address: Art Market "Kolekcija", Bokeška 11, Podgorica 81000

Directions: From the city center, embark on a leisurely stroll southwest along Njegoševa. As you reach the intersection with Bokeska, turn right. You'll soon encounter the captivating Art Market "Kolekcija" on your left. This market is a veritable treasure trove of Montenegrin artistry. Here, you'll find a rich array of handcrafted items, ranging from intricately designed ceramics to evocative paintings and sculptures, all of which showcase the depth of talent among local artists. Each piece tells a story, offering a tangible connection to Montenegro's vibrant artistic heritage.

For Foodies:

Gift/Souvenir: Local Wines and Spirits

Where to Get Them: Vukoje Cellar

Address: *Vukoje Cellar, Ulica Tolosi bb, Podgorica 81000*

Directions: Embark on a culinary adventure southwest from the city center along Njegoševa. As you reach Džordža Vašingtona Street, take a left turn. Follow the E65, and when you come across the exit toward Kuči, make the necessary turn. Merge onto the E80, and once again, look for the exit toward Kuči. Merge onto E65, and then turn left onto Ulica Tolosi. Behold, the Vukoje Cellar will grace your left. This is a sanctuary for wine connoisseurs and spirit enthusiasts alike. The cellar is home to a meticulously curated selection of Montenegrin wines and spirits, each bottle a testament to the region's viticultural heritage. From robust reds to delicate whites, and from fine brandies to aromatic liqueurs, the Vukoje Cellar offers a spectrum of flavors that capture the essence of Montenegro's winemaking tradition.

For History Buffs:

Gift/Souvenir: *Antique Maps and Books*

Where to Get Them: Antikvarnica "Znak"

Address: *Antikvarnica "Znak", Slobode 29, Podgorica 81000*

Directions: Begin your historical exploration by heading southwest along Njegoševa from the city center. As you arrive at Slobode Street, make a right turn. Lo and behold, Antikvarnica "Znak" will greet you on the right. This delightful antique shop is a veritable treasure trove for history aficionados. The shelves are adorned with vintage maps that unfurl tales of bygone eras, and the pages of rare books whisper secrets from centuries past. Stepping into this charming establishment is akin to embarking on a time-traveling adventure, as you peruse through artifacts that have witnessed the annals of history.

For Fashion and Jewelry Lovers:

Gift/Souvenir: Montenegrin Handmade Jewelry

Where to Get Them: Handmade Jewelry Store "Jewelry Emporium"

Address: Handmade Jewelry Store "Jewelry Emporium", Bokeska 9, Podgorica 81000

Directions: Begin your quest for exquisite jewelry by heading southwest along Njegoševa from the city center. As you arrive at Bokeska Street, turn left. Behold, the Jewelry Emporium will dazzle you on the right. This boutique store is a haven for those with an appreciation for the art of adornment. Here, you'll discover a stunning collection of handcrafted jewelry, each piece an expression of Montenegrin traditions and culture. From intricately designed necklaces to delicately crafted earrings, every item is a testament to the skill and artistry of local jewelers.

For Nature Enthusiasts:

Gift/Souvenir: Lavender and Herbal Products

Where to Get Them: "Podgorica Lavender Shop"

Address: "Podgorica Lavender Shop", Crnogorskih Serdara 5, Podgorica 81000

Directions: Set off on a fragrant journey southwest along Njegoševa from the city center. As you approach the intersection with Bokeska, turn right onto Crnogorskih Serdara. Lo and behold, the "Podgorica Lavender Shop" will greet you on the right. This charming shop is a sanctuary for nature enthusiasts and lovers of all things herbal. Here, you'll find a delightful array of lavender-based products, each infused with the soothing essence of this beloved plant. From fragrant sachets to soothing essential oils, the shop offers an aromatic journey through Montenegro's natural bounty.

BUDVA

Have you ever wondered about the captivating tales that echo through the ancient walls of Budva? Before we dive into the sun-kissed beaches and vibrant streets, let's uncover some intriguing fun facts about this coastal gem. Did you know that Budva is one of the oldest settlements along the Adriatic coast, with roots reaching back over two millennia? Its historic core, nestled on a peninsula, bears witness to the rise and fall of empires, making it a living museum of diverse cultures. Now, let's embark on a journey through the labyrinthine streets, golden beaches, and rich traditions that define the way of life in this enchanting Montenegrin town.

WHAT TO DO

For History Enthusiasts:

Budva Old Town (Stari Grad Budva)

Uniqueness: Stepping into Budva's Old Town is like entering a living museum. With origins dating back to ancient Greece, this well-preserved historic center is a testament to centuries of cultural exchange. The Venetian walls that embrace the town bear witness to its strategic importance throughout history. As you wander through its cobbled streets, you'll encounter ancient buildings, charming squares, and historic churches, including the Church of St. John and the Church of the Holy Trinity.

Directions: Upon entering Budva, follow the main road towards the coast. The Old Town is prominently situated on a peninsula, and you'll find several entrances leading into this enchanting historical district.

For Beach and Sun Seekers:

Mogren Beach

Uniqueness: Mogren Beach is a hidden gem nestled between rugged cliffs, accessible through a tunnel that adds an element of adventure to your visit. Once you emerge, you'll be greeted by a stunning panorama of the Adriatic Sea. The beach, divided into Mogren I and Mogren II, offers pebbly shores, clear azure waters, and an excellent view of the Budva Riviera.

Directions: Starting from the Old Town, follow the road that runs parallel to the coastline towards the southwest. Signs indicating "Mogren" will guide you to the entrance.

For Nature Lovers:

Sveti Stefan Island

Uniqueness: Sveti Stefan Island is a postcard-worthy destination, with its pink sandy beaches and quaint stone buildings perched on a small islet. The causeway connecting it to the mainland adds to the charm. Originally a fishing village, it's now home to a luxury resort, adding a touch of exclusivity to its natural beauty.

Directions: Follow the coastal road south from Budva's Old Town, and you'll encounter clear signs indicating the way to Sveti Stefan.

For Adventure Seekers:

Hiking in the Brajići Village

Uniqueness: Brajići offers a tranquil escape into the Montenegrin countryside. The village is surrounded by olive groves and boasts stunning vistas of the Budva Riviera. Hiking trails lead you through idyllic landscapes, providing ample opportunities for panoramic photographs.

Directions: From Budva, head northeast on the E65 towards Brajići. Once you arrive, you'll find signposts pointing towards various hiking routes.

For Nightlife Enthusiasts:

Budva Riviera Nightlife

Uniqueness: When the sun sets, Budva comes alive with an electric nightlife scene. From beachfront clubs like Top Hill to intimate bars in the Old Town, there's a venue for every taste. The atmosphere is charged with a mix of locals and tourists, creating a dynamic and vibrant ambiance.

Directions: Simply stroll along the Budva Riviera in the evening. The city center and beachfront areas are bustling with nightlife venues, making it easy to find a spot that suits your preferences.

WHERE TO STAY

Astoria Hotel & Spa

Unique Beauty: Astoria Hotel & Spa is a testament to the seamless fusion of contemporary elegance and Montenegrin heritage. The architectural design marries sleek lines with traditional elements, creating a captivating visual appeal. The highlight, however, is the rooftop terrace, where guests are treated to a panoramic spectacle of the Adriatic Sea and the enchanting Budva Old Town. The play of light on the sea at sunset is a sight to behold, making this terrace a cherished spot for both guests and locals alike. The spa, adorned with natural materials and calming hues, offers a sanctuary for rejuvenation, complementing the overall beauty of this establishment.

Dukley Hotel & Resort

Unique Beauty: Dukley Hotel & Resort exudes an air of refined luxury. Nestled within lush Mediterranean gardens, the resort is a visual feast, with vibrant flora complementing the azure backdrop of the Adriatic Sea. The private beach area is a true gem, where guests can bask in the beauty of Budva's coastline in an exclusive and tranquil setting. The architecture is a testament to the seamless integration of modern design with the natural beauty of the Budva Riviera. The structures seem to emerge from the landscape itself, creating a harmonious blend of nature and luxury.

Hotel Budva - Old Town

Unique Beauty: Hotel Budva - Old Town is a hidden gem within the historic walls of Budva's Old Town. The exterior exudes the charm of a medieval building, with stone walls that tell tales of centuries gone by. The interior, however, surprises with a blend of contemporary comfort and classic elegance. The rooftop terrace offers an unrivaled view of the

Adriatic Sea and the red-tiled roofs of the Old Town, creating a captivating contrast of colors and textures. Here, guests can immerse themselves in the timeless beauty of Budva, with the sea breeze carrying whispers of history.

Hotel Avala Resort & Villas

Unique Beauty: Hotel Avala Resort & Villas is a striking presence along the Budva waterfront. Its architectural design is nothing short of spectacular, featuring a cascading terrace structure that allows every room to enjoy unobstructed sea views. The infinity pool, perched on the edge of the cliff, seems to merge seamlessly with the Adriatic horizon. It's a vantage point that offers a profound appreciation for the beauty of the bay. The entire complex is a testament to the harmonious relationship between architecture and the natural surroundings, creating a visual masterpiece that captivates both guests and passersby.

Hotel Splendid Conference and Spa Resort

Unique Beauty: Hotel Splendid Conference and Spa Resort stands as a beacon of luxury on the Budva Riviera. The grandeur of its architectural design is awe-inspiring, creating an immediate sense of opulence. The interiors are adorned with lavish details, from crystal chandeliers to marble floors, creating an ambiance of regal splendor. The vast spa complex, complete with indoor pools, wellness facilities, and serene lounging areas, is a true sanctuary of tranquility. It's a place where guests can indulge in a world of beauty and relaxation, perfectly complementing the overall magnificence of this resort.

WHAT TO EAT

For Seafood Enthusiasts:

Restaurant: Porto

Must-Eat: The seafood platter at Porto is a true delight for seafood enthusiasts. It's a medley of the freshest catches from the Adriatic Sea, expertly prepared in the Mediterranean style. Grilled fish, calamari, mussels, and prawns are seasoned to perfection and served with a selection of local herbs and olive oil.

Must-Drink: Complement your seafood feast with a glass of local Vranac red wine. The robust flavors of Vranac, Montenegro's signature grape variety, pair beautifully with the richness of the seafood platter.

Directions: As you step out of the Old Town, follow the main road towards the marina. Porto is an elegant establishment located on the left-hand side, just before you reach the marina. Its proximity to the Old Town makes it an easily accessible culinary gem.

For Authentic Montenegrin Cuisine:

Restaurant: Konoba Stari Grad

Must-Eat: Konoba Stari Grad is renowned for its authentic Montenegrin flavors. The Ćevapi, a dish of grilled minced meat seasoned with local spices, is a staple here. Additionally, don't miss the Njeguški Steak, a delectable specialty originating from the nearby village of Njeguši.

Must-Drink: Pair your meal with a glass of Nikšićko Pivo, a popular local beer known for its crisp taste and refreshing quality.

Directions: Nestled within the Old Town, Konoba Stari Grad is a short walk from the main gate. As you wander through the charming alleys, follow the signs leading to Vuka Karadžića, where you'll discover this authentic culinary haven.

For Vegetarian and Vegan Options:

Restaurant: Green Paradise

Must-Eat: Green Paradise caters beautifully to vegetarian and vegan palates. The Vegan Buddha Bowl is a colorful and nutritious masterpiece, combining an array of fresh, plant-based ingredients. Additionally, the Spinach and Feta Stuffed Mushrooms offer a delightful burst of flavors.

Must-Drink: Enhance your dining experience with a freshly squeezed juice of the day, bursting with vitamins and natural goodness.

Directions: Situated just a short distance from the Old Town, Green Paradise is easily accessible. Follow Filipa Đuraškovića Street, where you'll find this oasis of green goodness on your right-hand side.

For International Flavors:

Restaurant: Konoba Dalmatino

Must-Eat: Konoba Dalmatino presents an enticing menu of international favorites. The Beef Bourguignon, a classic French dish, is a tender and flavorful choice. For a taste of Italy, the Spaghetti Carbonara is a creamy delight.

Must-Drink: Complement your meal with a glass of Montenegrin Prokupac red wine, known for its velvety texture and rich berry notes.

Directions: Within the Old Town, Konoba Dalmatino is a gem awaiting discovery. As you stroll along Vuka Karadžića Street, you'll find this charming establishment on your left, emanating the aromas of delectable international cuisine.

For Romantic Evenings:

Restaurant: Ambiente

Must-Eat: Ambiente is the perfect setting for a romantic evening. Indulge in the Lobster Risotto, a dish that marries the delicate sweetness of lobster with creamy Arborio rice. The Beef Tenderloin in Truffle Sauce is a symphony of flavors, offering a decadent culinary experience.

Must-Drink: Enhance the romance with a glass of Montenegrin Cabernet Sauvignon, known for its robust character and deep, fruity undertones.

Directions: Ambiente is nestled within the Old Town, exuding an atmosphere of romance. As you meander down Vuka Karadžića Street, this intimate restaurant beckons on your right, promising an unforgettable dining experience.

WHAT TO BRING HOME

For Art Enthusiasts:

Gift/Souvenir: Hand-Painted Ceramics

Description: The Art Atelier in Budva is a treasure trove for art enthusiasts. Here, you'll find a stunning collection of hand-painted ceramics, each piece a work of art in itself. The intricate designs and vibrant colors capture the essence of Montenegrin culture and craftsmanship. From decorative plates to ornate vases, these ceramics make for exquisite keepsakes or decorative pieces in any home.

Directions: As you explore the Old Town, make your way to Trg Slobode (Freedom Square). The Art Atelier is located here, easily recognizable by the colorful display of hand-painted ceramics in its storefront. It's a haven for art lovers seeking a piece of Budva's creative spirit.

For Foodies:

Gift/Souvenir: Local Olive Oil and Honey Products

Description: The Budva Farmer's Market is a haven for food enthusiasts looking for authentic Montenegrin flavors. Here, you'll find an array of local products, with olive oil and honey taking center stage. The olive oil is pressed from the finest local olives, boasting a rich and robust flavor. Meanwhile, the honey is sourced from the region's diverse flora, resulting in a delightful spectrum of tastes, from floral to herbal notes.

Directions: Head south from the Old Town along IV Proleterska, then turn left onto Topliški put. The Budva Farmer's Market is located along this road, offering a delightful selection of local delicacies, including olive oil and honey.

For History Buffs:

Gift/Souvenir: Replicas of Antique Coins and Artifacts

Description: As you wander through the Old Town of Budva, you'll come across various souvenir shops that specialize in replicas of antique coins, pottery, and historical artifacts. These items serve as tangible links to Budva's rich history, allowing history buffs to bring a piece of the past home. Whether it's a replica of a Roman coin or a miniature statue reminiscent of ancient times, these souvenirs are cherished keepsakes.

Directions: Explore the Old Town's narrow streets and alleys. You'll encounter numerous souvenir shops along the way, each offering a diverse selection of replicas of antique coins, pottery, and historical artifacts.

For Fashion and Jewelry Lovers:

Gift/Souvenir: Handmade Silver Jewelry

Description: Silver House in Budva is a treasure trove for those with a penchant for exquisite jewelry. Here, you'll find an extensive collection of handmade silver pieces, each crafted with precision and care. From intricate necklaces to elegant earrings, the designs are inspired by Montenegro's natural beauty and cultural heritage. These pieces make for timeless and cherished gifts, carrying a piece of Budva's craftsmanship with them.

Directions: Head southeast from the Old Town along IV Proleterska. Turn right onto Vuka Karadžića, and you'll find Silver House on your right. Its storefront is adorned with an enticing display of handmade silver jewelry.

For Nature Enthusiasts:

Gift/Souvenir: Lavender Products

Description: The Lavender Shop in Budva is a fragrant oasis for nature enthusiasts. Here, you'll discover a range of lavender-based products, from soothing oils to fragrant sachets. Lavender, a symbol of tranquility and natural beauty, is abundant in the region, and these products capture its essence perfectly. Whether it's for relaxation or as a delightful reminder of Budva's natural splendor, these lavender products are a wonderful choice.

Directions: From the Old Town, head south along IV Proleterska, then turn left onto Vuka Karadžića. The Lavender Shop Budva will be on your left, emanating the soothing scent of lavender.

HERCEG NOVI

Herceg Novi, nestled at the entrance of the Bay of Kotor, welcomes you with open arms. This charming coastal town is steeped in history, its story interwoven with the rise and fall of empires. Have you ever wondered about the tales etched into its ancient stone streets or the vibrant culture that thrives within its walls? Herceg Novi is a place where time seems to stand still, where the past and present coexist in harmony.

The town earned the affectionate moniker "City of a Thousand Steps" due to its winding alleys and steep staircases, offering breathtaking views at every turn. This unique topography is just one of the many facets that give Herceg Novi its character. As you wander through the streets, you'll encounter the echoes of Byzantine, Venetian, Ottoman, and Austro-Hungarian influences, a testament to its rich cultural heritage. This diversity is not only seen in the architecture but also in the cuisine and traditions that have been passed down through generations.

Founded in the 14th century, Herceg Novi has been a witness to the ebb and flow of empires. From being a fortified settlement to a strategic naval hub, its history is etched in the very stones that pave its streets. The town wears its history proudly, with ancient fortifications like Kanli Kula and graceful monasteries like Savina Monastery, all standing as living testaments to the past.

WHAT TO DO

For History Enthusiasts:

Kanli Kula (Bloody Tower)

Kanli Kula stands as a testament to Herceg Novi's turbulent past. Built during the Ottoman Empire's rule, its name harkens back to the conflicts that took place here. Today, the tower provides a captivating journey through history. Its sturdy stone walls house a small museum, where artifacts and exhibits shed light on the town's maritime heritage and the various civilizations that left their mark. Climbing to the top rewards visitors with a panoramic view of the Bay of Kotor, stretching out towards the open sea.

Directions: From the main square (Nikole Đurkovića), head southeast onto the seaside promenade (Pet Danica). Follow this path for about 200 meters, and you'll find the entrance to Kanli Kula on your right.

Savina Monastery

Savina Monastery is a haven of tranquility, nestled amidst lush greenery and commanding views of the azure waters below. The interior of the monastery is adorned with intricate frescoes, depicting scenes from the Bible. The peaceful atmosphere and well-tended gardens create a serene environment for reflection and contemplation. Additionally, the monastery's vineyards produce a renowned wine that has become an integral part of the local culture.

Directions: From the main square, head northeast along Njegoševa Street. After about 1 kilometer, take a right onto Put II Njeguša. Continue for another kilometer, and you'll reach Savina Monastery on your left.

For Nature Lovers:

Submarine Tunnels

The Submarine Tunnels offer a truly unique beach experience. Carved into the cliffs during World War II, these tunnels now provide natural shade and a sense of adventure for sunseekers. The crystal-clear waters surrounding the tunnels are perfect for snorkeling, offering a glimpse into the diverse marine life of the Adriatic. It's a place where history and nature harmoniously converge, providing a memorable day at the beach.

Directions: From the main square, head west on Njegoševa Street. After approximately 500 meters, you'll reach the beach area. Follow the path to the left, and you'll find the entrances to the tunnels.

Pet Danica Promenade

The Pet Danica Promenade is a leisurely path that skirts the coastline, inviting residents and visitors alike to bask in the beauty of the Adriatic. Lined with palm trees, benches, and sculptures, the promenade is perfect for a morning jog, a romantic sunset stroll, or simply sitting and watching the boats gently bob on the water. This iconic promenade encapsulates the relaxed Mediterranean way of life that Herceg Novi is known for.

Directions: Begin at the main square and head southeast onto Pet Danica. The promenade stretches along the coast, offering picturesque views of the sea.

For Art and Culture Aficionados:

Forte Mare Fortress

Forte Mare is a living piece of history, its stone walls having witnessed centuries of change. Throughout the year, the fortress transforms into a cultural hub, hosting a variety of events. From concerts under the starry Montenegrin sky to art exhibitions that blend modern creativity with ancient architecture, Forte Mare offers a dynamic space where the past and present converge in a vibrant celebration of culture.

Directions: From the main square, head southeast along Njegoševa Street. After about 300 meters, take a right onto Topliški put. Continue for another 100 meters, and you'll arrive at the entrance to Forte Mare on your left.

WHERE TO STAY

Palmon Bay Hotel & Spa:

Unique Beauty: Palmon Bay Hotel & Spa stands as a modern oasis along the Herceg Novi coastline. Its sleek architectural design is perfectly complemented by its proximity to the Adriatic Sea. The interior spaces are bathed in natural light, creating an inviting and serene atmosphere. The spa area, with its calming color palette and panoramic views, is a haven for relaxation.

Local Recommendations: Locals often praise the hotel's commitment to quality service. The spacious rooms and suites are elegantly furnished, providing a comfortable retreat for guests. The spa facilities, including the heated indoor pool, are highly regarded. Additionally, the hotel's beachfront location and proximity to the Old Town make it a convenient choice for exploring the town.

Perla Residence Hotel & SPA:

Unique Beauty: Perla Residence Hotel & SPA exudes a timeless elegance that pays homage to its historic surroundings. The stone façade, characteristic of the Old Town, sets the tone for a stay steeped in heritage. Inside, the interiors are a blend of rustic elements and contemporary comforts. The rooftop terrace, with its unobstructed views of the bay, provides a magical setting for relaxation.

Local Recommendations: Locals appreciate the hotel's commitment to preserving the architectural heritage of the Old Town. The rooms, adorned with traditional Montenegrin elements, offer a cozy and authentic experience. The rooftop terrace, often lauded for its enchanting sunsets, becomes a focal point for guests. The attentive staff and personalized service further enhance the overall experience.

Iberostar Herceg Novi:

Unique Beauty: Iberostar Herceg Novi is a retreat ensconced in nature's embrace. The terraced layout of the hotel allows for unobstructed views of the sparkling Adriatic Sea. Lush Mediterranean gardens surround the property, creating a tranquil atmosphere. The infinity pool seemingly merges with the horizon, providing a serene spot for relaxation.

Local Recommendations: Locals frequently commend Iberostar for its peaceful ambiance, making it an ideal escape from the hustle and bustle of daily life. The well-maintained gardens, complete with fragrant citrus trees, add to the overall allure. Guests often find themselves captivated by the breathtaking sea views from various vantage points around the hotel.

Hotel Casa del Mare - Amfora:

Unique Beauty: Hotel Casa del Mare - Amfora is a boutique gem that exudes an intimate and romantic atmosphere. The rooms are adorned with elegant furnishings, and nautical accents pay homage to the maritime heritage of the region. The beachfront location provides an enchanting backdrop for guests, and the terrace offers a serene spot to soak in the coastal ambiance.

Local Recommendations: Locals frequently highlight the personalized service at Hotel Casa del Mare - Amfora. The attention to detail in the design and decor is often lauded, creating a warm and inviting environment. The on-site restaurant, known for its delectable seafood dishes, is a favorite among guests. The hotel's proximity to the sea ensures that the soothing sounds of the waves are a constant companion.

Hotel Novi:

Unique Beauty: Hotel Novi boasts a prime location along the beachfront promenade, providing guests with easy access to the Adriatic Sea. The hotel's design emphasizes modern comfort, and the spacious terrace is a focal point for guests to relax and soak in the sea breeze. The interior spaces are bright and airy, creating a welcoming atmosphere.

Local Recommendations: Locals often recommend Hotel Novi for its family-friendly amenities and welcoming atmosphere. The spacious rooms cater to families, providing a comfortable and convenient stay. The hotel's beachfront location makes it an ideal choice for families looking to enjoy the sun and sea. The friendly staff, known for their warm hospitality, further enhance the overall experience.

WHAT TO EAT

Konoba Catovica Mlini (For Seafood Enthusiasts):

Must-Eat: The Grilled Seafood Platter at Konoba Catovica Mlini is a true delight for seafood enthusiasts. This generous platter features an array of freshly caught Adriatic seafood, perfectly grilled to highlight their natural flavors. From succulent fish to tender calamari, every bite is a taste of the pristine waters that surround Herceg Novi.

Must-Drink: Pairing this exquisite seafood platter with a local Montenegrin wine is a match made in culinary heaven. The wine list at Konoba Catovica Mlini offers a selection of high-quality Montenegrin vintages, perfectly complementing the rich flavors of the seafood.

Konoba Špina (For Traditional Montenegrin Cuisine):

Must-Eat: The Njeguški Steak at Konoba Špina is a culinary masterpiece that pays homage to Montenegro's rich gastronomic heritage. This dish features a succulent pork steak topped with smoked ham and cheese, creating a harmonious blend of flavors and textures. It's a true taste of Montenegrin tradition on a plate.

Must-Drink: To enhance the experience, try a glass of Montenegrin Rakija. This traditional fruit brandy is a beloved drink in the region and serves as the perfect accompaniment to the hearty and flavorful Njeguški Steak.

Stari Mlini (For International Flavors):

Must-Eat: The Duck Breast with Orange Sauce at Stari Mlini is a culinary revelation. The perfectly cooked duck breast, adorned with a tangy and aromatic orange sauce, creates a symphony of flavors that will tantalize your taste buds. It's a dish that showcases the culinary expertise of the chefs at Stari Mlini.

Must-Drink: At Stari Mlini, explore their craft beer selection. Pairing the duck with a well-chosen craft beer can elevate the dining experience, allowing you to savor the nuanced flavors and aromas in every sip.

Forte Rose Lounge Bar & Grill (For Vegetarians and Vegans):

Must-Eat: The Grilled Vegetables and Halloumi Cheese at Forte Rose is a delightful option for vegetarians and vegans. The combination of smoky grilled vegetables with the creamy and slightly salty halloumi cheese creates a harmonious and satisfying dish. It's a testament to how simple, quality ingredients can create a memorable culinary experience.

Must-Drink: Complement this dish with one of their freshly squeezed fruit juices. The vibrant and refreshing flavors of the juice pair wonderfully with the grilled vegetables and halloumi, creating a balanced and invigorating dining experience.

Conte Restaurant & Lounge (For Romantic Evenings):

Must-Eat: The Lobster Pasta at Conte is a dish fit for a romantic evening. The succulent lobster, delicately cooked and served with perfectly al dente pasta, is a celebration of the sea's bounty. The rich and aromatic flavors of this dish are sure to leave a lasting impression.

Must-Drink: Pairing the Lobster Pasta with a glass of Montenegrin red wine enhances the overall experience. The complex and robust notes of the wine complement the indulgent flavors of the dish, creating a memorable dining experience.

WHAT TO BRING HOME

For Art Enthusiasts:

Gift/Souvenir: Hand-Painted Ceramics

Where to Get Them: The "Herceg Novi Art Colony" is a treasure trove for art enthusiasts. Local artists showcase their hand-painted ceramics, each piece telling a unique story. Additionally, numerous artisan shops around Herceg Novi offer a wide selection of beautifully crafted ceramics.

Directions: As you head southwest along the seaside promenade from the main square, you'll find the Herceg Novi Art Colony and artisan shops scattered along the way. Look out for charming storefronts displaying these exquisite ceramics.

For Foodies:

Gift/Souvenir: Local Olive Oil and Honey Products

Where to Get Them: The bustling "Herceg Novi Marketplace" (Pijaca od Herceg Novi) is the go-to destination for foodies seeking local olive oil and honey products. Here, vendors proudly display an array of high-quality, locally sourced goods.

Directions: From the main square, continue southwest along the seaside promenade. After about 400 meters, you'll come across the Herceg Novi

Marketplace on your right. The vibrant stalls are hard to miss.

For History Buffs:

Gift/Souvenir: Antique Maps and Nautical Charts

Where to Get Them: The "Herceg Novi Old Town Antique Shop" is a treasure trove for history enthusiasts. Here, you'll find an exquisite collection of antique maps and nautical charts that harken back to the town's maritime legacy.

Directions: Head southeast onto Njegoševa Street from the main square. After about 200 meters, you'll encounter the entrance to the Old Town. The Herceg Novi Old Town Antique Shop is located on your left, a stone's throw from this historic entrance.

For Fashion and Jewelry Lovers:

Gift/Souvenir: Handmade Silver Jewelry

Where to Get Them: "Silver Moon" is a boutique jewelry store that caters to those with an appreciation for exquisite, handcrafted silver pieces. Here, you'll find an array of unique designs that capture the essence of Herceg Novi.

Directions: From the main square, continue southwest along the seaside promenade. After approximately 150 meters, you'll find Silver Moon on your right. The store's captivating window displays often catch the eye of passersby.

For Nature Enthusiasts:

Gift/Souvenir: Lavender Products

Where to Get Them: The "Herceg Novi Lavender Shop" is a haven for nature enthusiasts. Lavender-based products, ranging from essential oils to sachets, offer a fragrant reminder of Herceg Novi's natural beauty.

Directions: As you continue southwest along the seaside promenade from the main square, look for the Herceg Novi Lavender Shop after about 300 meters on your left. The inviting scent of lavender may guide you to this charming boutique.

TIVAT

Tivat, nestled along the beautiful Bay of Kotor in Montenegro, is a town of unique charm and stunning natural beauty. With its rich history, picturesque landscapes, and modern amenities, Tivat has become a sought-after destination for travelers seeking a perfect blend of culture, relaxation, and adventure.

The town's history dates back to ancient times when it was known as Teute and was an important settlement of the Illyrian Queen Teuta. Over the centuries, it passed through various hands, including the Venetians and the Austro-Hungarian Empire, leaving behind a tapestry of architectural styles that now grace the town.

Today, Tivat is known for its flourishing marina, Porto Montenegro, which has earned a reputation as one of the premier yachting destinations in the Mediterranean. With its luxurious facilities, high-end boutiques, and top-notch restaurants, Porto Montenegro draws in a cosmopolitan crowd from around the world.

Beyond the marina, Tivat offers a range of attractions for visitors. The Naval Heritage Collection is a notable museum, housing an impressive array of maritime artifacts that trace the region's seafaring history. Additionally, the Renaissance Summer House Buca is a splendid example of Venetian architecture, offering a glimpse into the town's historic past.

Nature enthusiasts will find Tivat equally captivating. The town is surrounded by lush green hills, perfect for hiking and exploration. The solace of the nearby Gornja Lastva village provides a tranquil retreat for those seeking a break from the bustle of modern life.

For beach lovers, Tivat offers a selection of pristine beaches along the Adriatic coast. Gradska Plaža, or Town Beach, is a popular spot for locals and visitors alike, offering stunning views of the bay and a vibrant atmosphere. The nearby Plavi Horizonti, with its soft sands and crystal-clear waters, is another gem for sun-seekers.

The cuisine in Tivat is a delightful fusion of Mediterranean and Balkan flavors. Local restaurants serve up an array of fresh seafood, olives, cheeses, and wines, creating a gastronomic experience that complements the town's coastal ambiance.

In essence, Tivat is a town that effortlessly marries its rich history with modern elegance..

WHAT TO DO

For Yachting Enthusiasts:

Visit Porto Montenegro

Uniqueness: Porto Montenegro is not just a marina; it's a lifestyle destination that marries luxury and nautical elegance. It's a haven for yacht owners and enthusiasts, offering world-class berthing, state-of-the-art facilities, and a vibrant social scene. The marina promenade is lined with high-end boutiques, restaurants, and bars, creating a cosmopolitan atmosphere.

Year Founded: The transformation of the former naval base into Porto Montenegro began in 2006. Since then, it has become a beacon for the global yachting community.

Directions: From the town center, head towards the waterfront. As you approach the coast, you'll find yourself at the entrance to Porto Montenegro. Follow the promenade, and you'll be immersed in the glamorous world of yachting.

For History Buffs:

Explore Naval Heritage Collection

Uniqueness: The Naval Heritage Collection is a treasure trove for history enthusiasts. It houses an extensive collection of maritime artifacts, each with its own story to tell about Montenegro's naval legacy. From meticulously crafted ship models to vintage naval uniforms, the museum provides a window into the region's seafaring heritage.

Year Founded: The museum opened its doors in 2012, offering a comprehensive insight into Montenegro's maritime history.

Directions: As you head towards the marina from the town center, enter the Porto Montenegro complex. The Naval Heritage Collection is located within the complex, adjacent to the waterfront.

For Nature Lovers:

Hike to Vrmac Peninsula

Uniqueness: The Vrmac Peninsula is a nature lover's paradise. It offers a network of trails that wind through diverse Mediterranean vegetation, leading to panoramic viewpoints. The views of the Bay of Kotor and Tivat from the peninsula are nothing short of spectacular.

Directions: From the town center, make your way towards the base of Vrmac Peninsula. Look for signposts indicating the hiking trails, and follow them as they lead you through the lush landscape.

For Beachgoers:

Relax at Plavi Horizonti Beach

Uniqueness: Plavi Horizonti, nestled in a picturesque cove, is a sanctuary for beach lovers. Its golden sands and crystal-clear waters provide an idyllic setting for relaxation and aquatic activities. The beach's intimate atmosphere sets it apart from larger, more crowded beaches in the region.

Directions: Plavi Horizonti Beach is located a short drive south of the town center. Follow the signs along the Adriatic Highway, and you'll reach the beach in no time.

For Architecture Aficionados:

Visit Buća-Luković Renaissance Summer House

Uniqueness: This beautifully preserved Renaissance summer house stands as a testament to Tivat's historic architectural heritage. With Venetian influences evident in its design, it offers a glimpse into the town's affluent past. The house's intricate details and timeless elegance make it a must-visit for architecture enthusiasts.

Year Founded: The Buća-Luković House dates back to the 17th century, showcasing the enduring legacy of Tivat's architectural history.

Directions: From the town center, head towards the marina. The Buća-Luković House is located in the heart of Tivat's historic district, not far from the waterfront. Look for signs indicating its presence.

WHERE TO STAY

Hotel Regent Porto Montenegro

Unique Beauty: Hotel Regent Porto Montenegro is a beacon of luxury in Tivat. Its architectural elegance mirrors the glamour of the nearby marina, offering a seamless blend of modern sophistication and coastal charm. The hotel's design embraces the nautical heritage of the region, with sleek lines and maritime-inspired décor. The lush Mediterranean gardens surrounding the property add a touch of natural beauty to the overall ambiance.

La Roche Hotel

Unique Beauty: La Roche Hotel is a gem in Tivat's accommodation landscape. Housed in a meticulously restored stone building, the hotel exudes an old-world charm that harmonizes with the town's historic character. The inner courtyard, adorned with greenery and traditional features, provides a tranquil oasis for guests to relax in. This intimate setting allows for a truly immersive experience in Tivat's architectural heritage.

Hotel Pine

Unique Beauty: Hotel Pine is a sanctuary of natural beauty and tranquility. Its location in Gornja Lastva, surrounded by verdant hills and overlooking the bay, offers guests a retreat from the hustle and bustle of urban life. The hotel's architecture pays homage to traditional Montenegrin style, with stone façades and wooden accents. The well-tended gardens and terraces provide panoramic vistas, making it an ideal spot for nature enthusiasts.

Eco Hotel Carrubba

Unique Beauty: Eco Hotel Carrubba stands out for its commitment to sustainability and eco-conscious practices. The architecture seamlessly integrates with the natural surroundings of Donja Lastva. The use of local materials and renewable energy sources complements the hotel's ecological ethos. The tranquil garden, planted with native flora, showcases the beauty of Montenegro's natural landscape right at the doorstep.

Palma Hotel

Unique Beauty: Palma Hotel is a harmonious blend of modern comfort and Montenegrin hospitality. Its façade, adorned with traditional stone elements, nods to the town's architectural heritage. Inside, contemporary design and amenities provide a comfortable and convenient stay. The hotel's proximity to the waterfront allows guests to easily immerse themselves in Tivat's vibrant coastal atmosphere.

WHAT TO EAT

Tara Restaurant

Must-Eat: The Black Risotto with Seafood at Tara Restaurant is a culinary masterpiece. The risotto is rich and flavorful, with perfectly cooked seafood infused with the distinctive taste of cuttlefish ink.

Must-Drink: Pairing this dish with a glass of local Montenegrin Vranac Red Wine is a perfect complement. The robust and full-bodied notes of the wine enhance the flavors of the seafood in the risotto.

Directions: Tara Restaurant is nestled within the picturesque Porto Montenegro. As you approach the marina, follow the waterfront promenade. The restaurant, easily identifiable by its charming terrace, awaits with its delectable offerings.

Prova Restaurant & Lounge

Must-Eat: The Beef Carpaccio with Truffle Oil and Parmesan at Prova is a symphony of flavors. The tender beef, drizzled with truffle-infused oil and adorned with delicate Parmesan shavings, creates a melt-in-the-mouth experience.

Must-Drink: Sipping on the Signature Prova Cocktail is a delightful way to complement the meal. Crafted with precision, it offers a refreshing and harmonious blend of flavors.

Directions: Prova Restaurant & Lounge is perched on the waterfront, offering breathtaking views of the bay. As you approach Porto Montenegro, look for the elegant setting of Prova, where culinary excellence meets scenic beauty.

Konoba Bacchus

Must-Eat: The Grilled Octopus with Garlic and Olive Oil at Konoba Bacchus is a Mediterranean delight. The octopus is expertly cooked to tender perfection and complemented by the aromatic infusion of garlic and olive oil.

Must-Drink: Savoring this dish with a chilled Montenegrin Nikšićko Pivo (Beer) provides a refreshing contrast to the robust flavors of the octopus.

Directions: Konoba Bacchus exudes a relaxed atmosphere, making it a wonderful spot to unwind. Follow the path towards the marina, and you'll find this gem nestled within Porto Montenegro, offering a taste of authentic Montenegrin cuisine.

One Restaurant & Lounge Bar

Must-Eat: The Tuna Tartare with Avocado and Soy Sauce at One Restaurant & Lounge Bar is a symphony of textures and flavors. The freshness of the tuna, combined with the creamy avocado and zesty soy sauce, creates a harmonious culinary experience.

Must-Drink: The One Signature Cocktail, crafted by the skilled mixologists, is a testament to the creativity and artistry that defines this restaurant.

Directions: One Restaurant & Lounge Bar embodies a stylish and contemporary ambiance. As you approach the marina, seek out the chic setting of One, where modern cuisine meets elegant design.

Vino Santo Wine & Tapas Bar

Must-Eat: Indulge in a carefully curated Cheese and Charcuterie Platter at Vino Santo. This selection of cheeses and cured meats is expertly paired, offering a delightful combination of flavors and textures.

Must-Drink: Explore the extensive wine selection, both local and international, at Vino Santo. The knowledgeable staff can help you find the perfect wine to complement your tapas.

Directions: Vino Santo is nestled in Porto Montenegro Village, offering a cozy and intimate setting. Follow the waterfront promenade and look for the inviting ambiance of Vino Santo, where wine and tapas take center stage.

WHAT TO BRING HOME

Nautical-themed Souvenirs

Unique Feature: Tivat's maritime history is deeply ingrained in its culture, making nautical-themed souvenirs highly sought after. These can include items like ship models, sailor's knots, compasses, and marine-themed home decor.

Where to Get Them: Along the waterfront promenade, you'll find an array of shops catering to maritime enthusiasts. Stores like "Marine Gift Shop" in Porto Montenegro offer a wide selection of high-quality nautical-themed items.

Directions to Marine Gift Shop: Upon reaching the waterfront, follow the promenade towards Porto Montenegro. Keep an eye out for "Marine Gift Shop," which is usually located near the marina.

Traditional Montenegrin Clothing and Accessories

Unique Feature: Montenegrin clothing, including embroidered vests, hats, and accessories, showcase the country's rich cultural heritage. These items are often handmade and adorned with intricate patterns.

Where to Get Them: Boutiques and shops specializing in traditional attire are scattered throughout Tivat. "Boutique Montenegro" in the town center is a reputable spot for authentic Montenegrin clothing.

Directions to Boutique Montenegro: As you head from the waterfront towards the town center, walk along the main street. You'll easily spot "Boutique Montenegro" with its traditional clothing displays.

Handcrafted Jewelry

Unique Feature: Tivat boasts a vibrant community of jewelers who craft exquisite pieces using local gemstones and precious metals. These unique, one-of-a-kind pieces make for exceptional souvenirs.

Where to Get Them: Jewelry stores in the town center are the go-to places for finding handcrafted gems. "Adagio Jewelry" is a renowned shop with a diverse collection of beautifully crafted jewelry.

Directions to Adagio Jewelry: Head inland from the waterfront towards the town center. "Adagio Jewelry" is prominently located along the main street, displaying a stunning array of handcrafted pieces.

Local Art and Paintings

Unique Feature: Tivat's scenic landscapes and coastal beauty have long been an inspiration for local artists. Paintings capturing the essence of Montenegro's natural beauty are a cherished souvenir.

Where to Get Them: Art galleries and studios in town showcase a wide range of artworks. "Art House" is a notable gallery with an extensive collection of paintings, sculptures, and crafts.

Directions to Art House: As you move from the waterfront towards the town center, look for "Art House" along the main street. The gallery is a treasure trove of beautiful artworks representing the local culture and scenery.

Montenegrin Wines and Spirits

Unique Feature: Montenegro is gaining recognition for its burgeoning wine industry, producing high-quality vintages. Local wines and spirits provide an authentic taste of the region.

Where to Get Them: Wine shops and cellars are the best places to explore Montenegrin wines. "Monte Vino" in the town center offers a well-curated selection of fine Montenegrin vintages.

Directions to Monte Vino: From the waterfront, head towards the town center. "Monte Vino" is located along the main street and is easily identifiable by its collection of fine Montenegrin wines.

ULCINJ

Ulcinj, often known as the "Pearl of the Adriatic," is a charming coastal town in Montenegro, situated at the southernmost tip of the country. It boasts a diverse landscape, with the Adriatic Sea to the west and Lake Shkodër to the east, offering a unique blend of coastal and inland beauty. This strategic location has played a significant role in Ulcinj's

Directions to Ulcinj:

From Podgorica:

- Head southeast on the E65 highway.
- Continue on the E65 until you reach a junction for Ulcinj.
- Follow the signs leading to Ulcinj.

From Dubrovnik (Croatia):

- Take the E80 and E65 highways south toward the Montenegrin border.
- After crossing the border, continue on the E80/E851.
- Follow the signs to Ulcinj.

From Tirana (Albania):

- Head north on the SH2 highway toward the Albanian-Montenegrin border.
- After crossing the border, continue on the E851.
- Follow the signs to Ulcinj.

history, facilitating trade and cultural exchange over the centuries.

With a history spanning over 2,000 years, Ulcinj has witnessed the presence of ancient Illyrian and Roman settlements, as well as the influence of various civilizations, including the Byzantines, Venetians, Ottomans, and Austro-Hungarians. This rich historical tapestry is evident in the town's architecture, cuisine, and language. Notably, Ulcinj was a hub for Adriatic pirates during the medieval period.

The town's cultural diversity is a hallmark of its heritage, with a blend of Montenegrin, Albanian, and other ethnic communities shaping its character. This fusion is reflected in the local cuisine, which harmoniously combines Mediterranean and Balkan flavors. The traditional music and dance of Ulcinj also mirror this rich cultural heritage, incorporating elements from both Eastern and Western traditions.

Economically, Ulcinj has historically relied on fishing, agriculture, and trade, owing to its coastal and strategic location. In recent decades, tourism has emerged as a major driver of the local economy, drawing visitors with its pristine beaches, historic sites, and natural beauty. Additionally, agriculture remains a vital sector, with the region gaining recognition for its olive oil production and citrus fruits.

Tourists flock to Ulcinj for its stunning beaches, particularly Velika Plaza, which stretches over 13 kilometers. The Ada Bojana Island, formed by the delta of the Bojana River, stands as a unique natural reserve and a popular destination for water sports enthusiasts. The Old Town of Ulcinj, characterized by well-preserved medieval architecture, narrow cobbled streets, and historic mosques, offers a captivating glimpse into the town's storied past. Meanwhile, the Ulcinj Salinas, a protected nature reserve, serve as a sanctuary for birdwatchers, hosting numerous species of migratory birds.

In summation, Ulcinj's rich historical legacy, breathtaking natural landscapes, and vibrant cultural diversity make it a true gem on the Adriatic coast.

WHAT TO DO

Velika Plaza Beach (Great Beach):

For Beach Enthusiasts

Velika Plaza is renowned not only for its length but also for its stunning beauty. The soft golden sands stretch for over 13 kilometers along the Adriatic coast. The beach gently slopes into the azure waters, making it ideal for swimming and water sports such as jet-skiing and parasailing. Additionally, there are numerous beach bars and restaurants along the promenade where visitors can relax and savor local delicacies.

Directions from the city center: From Ulcinj's city center, follow the main road signs towards "Velika Plaza" or "Great Beach." It's a short drive or a pleasant walk depending on your preference.

Ada Bojana Island:

For Nature and Water Sports Enthusiasts

Ada Bojana, formed by the delta of the Bojana River, is a unique and tranquil natural reserve. The island is known for its lush vegetation, sandy shores, and an array of wildlife. It's a haven for water sports enthusiasts, particularly kite surfers and windsurfers due to its consistent winds. Birdwatching is also a popular activity here, with over 240 bird species recorded in the area.

Directions from the city center: Follow signs for Ada Bojana from the city center, and after a short drive, you'll reach a bridge leading to the island. There are also boat tours available if you prefer a scenic cruise.

Old Town (Stari Grad):

For History and Architecture Aficionados

Ulcinj's Old Town is a treasure trove of historical and architectural wonders. Encircled by ancient walls, the town's narrow cobbled streets lead to charming squares and centuries-old buildings. The Balsica Tower and the impressive Old Town Mosque are must-see landmarks. Cafes and shops line the streets, offering a taste of local life amidst this living museum.

Directions from Velika Plaza Beach: The Old Town is a short drive or a leisurely walk from Velika Plaza. Follow the signs or ask locals for directions.

Ulcinj Salinas:

For Birdwatchers and Nature Lovers

The Ulcinj Salinas, a protected nature reserve, is a serene sanctuary for nature enthusiasts. The salt flats, surrounded by breathtaking landscapes, provide a haven for over 250 bird species, including flamingos. Visitors can explore the area via marked trails, allowing for a peaceful immersion in nature.

Directions from the city center: Head towards Ada Bojana, and you'll find signs leading to Ulcinj Salinas. It's a short drive from the city center.

Olive Tree of Mirovica:

For Nature and Cultural Enthusiasts

The ancient Olive Tree of Mirovica is a living testament to the region's rich agricultural heritage. Estimated to be over 2,000 years old, this remarkable tree is a symbol of endurance and resilience. Visitors can stroll around the groves, appreciating the ancient olive trees and learning about their cultural significance.

Directions from the city center: Head inland from the city center towards the village of Mirovica. Follow the signs for the Olive Tree, and you'll arrive at this historic site.

WHERE TO STAY

Hotel Azul:

For Beach Lovers and Comfort Seekers

Hotel Azul is a gem for those who want to wake up to the soothing sound of waves and have the beach just steps away. The rooms are elegantly designed with a contemporary touch, offering all the modern amenities one could desire. The sea-facing balconies provide breathtaking views of the Adriatic, creating a serene atmosphere for relaxation. The on-site restaurant is celebrated for its fresh seafood dishes, which are often praised by both locals and visitors alike.

Villa Elena:

For History and Culture Enthusiasts

Nestled within the ancient walls of Ulcinj's Old Town, Villa Elena transports guests back in time. The meticulously restored stone architecture, complemented by tasteful furnishings, creates an enchanting atmosphere. The rooftop terrace is a highlight, offering panoramic views of the town and the sea. Guests can immerse themselves in the rich history of the area while enjoying modern comforts.

Ada Bojana Resort:

For Nature and Water Sports Enthusiasts

Ada Bojana Resort is a haven for nature lovers and adventure seekers. Set amidst the tranquil surroundings of Ada Bojana Island, guests can enjoy the harmonious blend of river, sea, and untouched nature. The resort offers a range of water sports activities, and the accommodations, including comfortable bungalows and villas, provide a cozy retreat after a day of outdoor adventure.

Hotel Palata Venezia:

For Romantic Getaways and History Buffs

This boutique hotel is a testament to Ulcinj's rich history, as it's housed in a beautifully restored Venetian palace. The romantic ambiance is palpable, from the charming courtyard to the elegantly appointed rooms. Couples can savor intimate moments in this enchanting setting. The restaurant, known for its delectable local cuisine, adds an extra layer of allure to the overall experience.

Olive Tree Hotel:

For Nature Lovers and Wellness Seekers

Surrounded by ancient olive groves, the Olive Tree Hotel offers a peaceful retreat for those seeking tranquility. The hotel's garden and swimming pool area are perfect for unwinding and soaking up the natural beauty. The rooms are designed with a soothing aesthetic, providing a comfortable and relaxing environment. Despite its serene location, the town center and beaches are easily accessible by a short drive.

WHAT TO EAT

Restaurant Antigona:

For Seafood Aficionados

Nestled near the historic Old Town, Restaurant Antigona is a gem for seafood lovers. The chefs here take pride in sourcing the freshest catches from the Adriatic Sea. One must-try dish is the Grilled Adriatic Sea Bass, which is expertly seasoned and cooked to perfection. Additionally, the Black Risotto with Cuttlefish Ink is a local delicacy that's not to be missed. To complement your meal, consider pairing it with a crisp, local white wine like Vranac, known for its pleasant acidity and fruity notes.

Directions from the city center: From the heart of Ulcinj, head south towards the Old Town. Once you reach the entrance of the Old Town, you'll find

Restaurant Antigona nestled along the charming streets.

Misko Fish Restaurant:

For Authentic Seafood Dining

Misko Fish Restaurant is a family-owned establishment that has earned a reputation for its genuine Montenegrin seafood offerings. The Grilled Octopus is a standout, known for its tender texture and rich flavor. For those seeking a variety of flavors, the Seafood Platter is an excellent choice, showcasing the best catches of the day. To complete your dining experience, indulge in a taste of the local Rakija, a traditional fruit brandy that embodies the essence of Montenegro.

Directions from the city center: Heading south along the coast towards Velika Plaza Beach, you'll find Misko Fish Restaurant situated along the beachfront. Look out for its inviting terrace and distinctive seaside ambiance.

Kod Milana:

For Balkan and Mediterranean Fusion

Kod Milana offers a delightful fusion of Balkan and Mediterranean cuisines. The Lamb and Potato Bake is a hearty and flavorful dish, showcasing the culinary prowess of the kitchen. If you're in the mood for seafood, the Seafood Pasta is a delectable choice, combining the freshness of the sea with Mediterranean herbs and spices. Enhance your dining experience with a glass of local red wine, such as Plantaze Vranac, known for its robust character and deep red color.

Directions from the city center: As you make your way towards Velika Plaza Beach, you'll find Kod Milana located along the main road leading to the beach. Its inviting facade and warm ambiance welcome guests for a memorable dining experience.

Bar Restaurant Viriato:

For International Flavors and Cocktails

Viriato stands out for its diverse menu, incorporating influences from around the world. The Beef Tenderloin with Truffle Sauce is a culinary masterpiece, offering a harmonious blend of flavors and textures. Vegetarians will appreciate the Vegetarian Moussaka, a flavorful and satisfying dish. To elevate your dining experience, explore the creative cocktail menu, with the Viriato Martini being a standout favorite.

Directions from the city center: Situated within the Old Town, Bar Restaurant Viriato is a delightful find. Follow the signs leading to the Old Town and you'll be guided to this charming establishment within the historic walls.

Restaurant Pjaca:

For Traditional Balkan Cuisine

Pjaca is a culinary haven for those seeking authentic Balkan flavors. The Grilled Platter with Various Meats is a carnivore's delight, showcasing the mastery of local grilling techniques. For a taste of Balkan comfort food, the Goulash is a must-try, with its rich, slow-cooked flavors. To complement your meal, enjoy a glass of Nikšićko Pivo, a beloved Montenegrin beer known for its crispness and refreshing taste.

Directions from the city center: Nestled in the heart of the Old Town, Restaurant Pjaca is easily accessible. Simply follow the signs leading to the Old Town, and you'll soon discover this charming eatery amidst the historic streets.

WHAT TO BRING HOME
Olive Oil and Olive-Based Products:

For Food and Culinary Enthusiasts

Ulcinj is renowned for its high-quality olive oil. You can find an array of olive-based products like flavored oils, soaps, and cosmetics. Visit local markets or specialized stores such as "Olive Land" (address: Stanka Dragojevića 3) or "Olive Oil Bar" (address: Velika Plaza) for a wide selection.

Directions from the city center: Both "Olive Land" and "Olive Oil Bar" are easily accessible from the city center. From the heart of Ulcinj, head towards Velika Plaza Beach. Both shops are situated along this route.

Handmade Jewelry and Accessories:

For Fashion and Jewelry Enthusiasts

Ulcinj boasts a vibrant artisan community creating unique jewelry pieces. Look for handmade earrings, necklaces, and bracelets crafted from semi-precious stones, shells, and metals. Head to the Old Town area, where you'll find numerous boutiques and stalls offering these artisanal treasures.

Directions from the city center: From the heart of Ulcinj, follow the signs leading to the Old Town. Within the historic walls, you'll discover a plethora of boutiques and artisan stalls offering a diverse range of jewelry.

Traditional Clothing and Textiles:

For Art and Culture Lovers

Ulcinj's Old Town is a treasure trove for those interested in traditional Montenegrin clothing and textiles. Look for hand-embroidered scarves, shawls, and clothing items made from high-quality materials. Shops like "Bazar Sud" (address: Stari Grad 47) and "Art Studio Minjon" (address: Stari Grad) are renowned for their exquisite textiles.

Directions from the city center: Both "Bazar Sud" and "Art Studio Minjon" are situated within the Old Town. Follow the signs leading to the Old Town and you'll encounter these establishments along the historic streets.

Local Artwork and Paintings:

For Art and Design Aficionados

Ulcinj's artistic community is vibrant, and you can find a range of paintings and artworks depicting local landscapes, culture, and traditions. Galleries like "Gallery Rame" (address: Stari Grad 2) and

"Gallery Liman" (address: Liman 1) showcase a diverse selection of artworks.

Directions from the city center: Both "Gallery Rame" and "Gallery Liman" are located within the Old Town. Follow the signs leading to the Old Town, and you'll find these galleries along the historic streets.

Local Handcrafted Souvenirs:

For Collectors and Travelers

Look for unique handcrafted souvenirs such as wooden carvings, pottery, and woven items. These can be found in various shops and market stalls throughout Ulcinj, particularly in the Old Town area.

Directions from the city center: Explore the Old Town area to find numerous shops and market stalls offering a wide array of handcrafted souvenirs. Follow the signs leading to the Old Town to discover these hidden gems.

CETINJE

Cetinje, often known as the "Old Royal Capital of Montenegro," is a historic town located in the heart of the Balkans. Nestled at the foot of Mount Lovćen, it holds significant cultural and political importance in Montenegro's history. This town's strategic position provides breathtaking views of the surrounding mountains, creating a serene and picturesque atmosphere. Additionally, Cetinje's proximity to the Adriatic coast, approximately 30 kilometers away, adds to its allure as a cultural and natural gem.

With roots tracing back to the 15th century, Cetinje served as the historical capital of Montenegro. It witnessed pivotal events in the nation's development, including the rule of the Petrović-Njegoš dynasty. Cetinje played a crucial role in Montenegro's struggle for independence and was central in shaping the country's political landscape. The town's museums, libraries, and historic buildings stand as tangible remnants of this rich historical legacy.

Cetinje is a melting pot of Montenegrin and European cultural influences. Its architecture showcases a harmonious blend of Venetian, Austro-

Hungarian, and Ottoman styles, while its museums house invaluable artifacts and artworks. The Cetinje Monastery, Biljarda (former residence of Petar II Petrović Njegoš), and the National Museum of Montenegro are among the notable cultural sites. The annual Cetinje Cultural Summer festival further underscores the vibrant artistic traditions of the region.

Economically, Cetinje serves as an administrative and educational hub, hosting government institutions, embassies, and the University of Montenegro. Tourism has also emerged as a significant contributor to the local economy, with visitors drawn to the town's rich cultural and historical heritage.

For tourists, Cetinje's appeal lies in its historical and cultural treasures. The town's museums, including the Museum of King Nikola and the Ethnographic Museum, offer a window into Montenegro's past. Additionally, the Lovćen National Park, with its striking mausoleum and scenic hiking trails, provides panoramic views of the Bay of Kotor. The blend of historical immersion and natural beauty creates a distinctive and compelling experience for travelers.

In essence, Cetinje encapsulates Montenegro's historical journey. Its rich cultural tapestry, set against a backdrop of awe-inspiring mountains, invites exploration into the heart of Balkan heritage.

Directions to Cetinje:

From Podgorica:

- Head west on the E65 highway towards Cetinje.
- Follow the signs leading to Cetinje, which is approximately 35 kilometers away from Podgorica.

From Kotor:

- Take the E80 and E65 highways north towards Cetinje.
- Follow the signs leading to Cetinje, approximately 35 kilometers away from Kotor.

From Dubrovnik (Croatia):

- Take the E65 highway east towards the Montenegrin border.
- After crossing the border, continue on the E65 towards Cetinje, which is about 40 kilometers away from the border.

WHAT TO DO

Cetinje Monastery (Cetinjski Manastir):

For History and Religious Enthusiasts

Founded in the 15th century, Cetinje Monastery is a cornerstone of Montenegrin spirituality. The monastery complex features a stunning church adorned with intricate frescoes, a richly decorated iconostasis, and a serene courtyard. The museum houses an impressive collection of religious artifacts, including ancient manuscripts and relics. Pilgrims and history buffs alike will appreciate the spiritual and cultural significance of this sacred site.

Njegoš Mausoleum:

For Cultural and Nature Enthusiasts

Perched atop Mount Lovćen, the mausoleum is a testament to Montenegro's reverence for Petar II Petrović Njegoš. Visitors embark on a picturesque drive through Lovćen National Park, ascending to an altitude of 1,657 meters. The mausoleum's striking architecture and panoramic terrace offer breathtaking views of the Bay of Kotor, creating a blend of cultural appreciation and natural wonder.

King Nikola's Palace (Biljarda):

For History and Architecture Aficionados

A visit to King Nikola's Palace provides a window into Montenegro's royal history. The elegant villa, reminiscent of European palatial architecture, transports visitors to a bygone era. The interior is adorned with period furniture, personal effects, and historical photographs. Exploring the palace offers a vivid glimpse into the opulent lifestyle of Montenegro's last reigning king.

Vladimir Vysotsky Monument:

For Art and Poetry Admirers

Nestled in a serene park, the Vladimir Vysotsky Monument pays homage to the enduring cultural ties between Montenegro and Russia. The bronze statue captures the spirit of the revered Russian poet and singer. The tranquil setting offers a moment of reflection, emphasizing the shared artistic heritage between the two nations.

Museum of King Nikola:

For History and Art Lovers

Housed in a splendid villa, the Museum of King Nikola provides an immersive journey into Montenegro's royal past. The exhibits showcase a wide array of artifacts, portraits, and documents related to the Petrović-Njegoš dynasty. Visitors can delve into the personal and historical narratives of Montenegro's monarchy, offering a deeper understanding of the nation's heritage.

WHERE TO STAY

Hotel Grand:

Location: Situated in the heart of Cetinje, Hotel Grand offers easy access to the main attractions of the town. It's just a short walk away from places like the Cetinje Monastery and the National Museum of Montenegro.

Accommodation: The hotel provides a range of rooms, from standard to deluxe, all tastefully decorated and equipped with modern amenities. Some rooms even offer views of the Lovćen Mountain.

Facilities: Hotel Grand boasts a restaurant serving local and international cuisine, a bar, and a terrace where guests can relax. There's also free Wi-Fi and parking available.

Hotel Monte Rosa:

Location: This charming hotel is located in a quiet residential area of Cetinje, providing a peaceful atmosphere for guests. It's still within walking distance of the town center.

Accommodation: The rooms at Hotel Monte Rosa are cozy and well-maintained. They offer a comfortable retreat after a day of exploring. Some rooms have balconies with lovely views.

Facilities: The hotel features a restaurant serving delicious Montenegrin dishes, and a garden where guests can unwind. The staff is known for their warm hospitality.

Hotel Ivanov Konak:

Location: Housed in a beautifully restored 18th-century palace, Hotel Ivanov Konak is a unique accommodation option in Cetinje. It's centrally located, close to historical sites and cultural attractions.

Accommodation: The rooms in this hotel exude old-world charm while still offering modern comforts. Guests can enjoy the elegant furnishings and period-appropriate decor.

Facilities: The hotel features a courtyard garden where guests can relax, and a lounge area for socializing. The ambiance here is steeped in history.

Villa Primavera:

Location: Villa Primavera is nestled in a serene part of Cetinje, surrounded by greenery. This location provides a peaceful and relaxing environment.

Accommodation: The villa offers spacious and comfortable rooms with tasteful decor. Some rooms have balconies or terraces overlooking the garden.

Facilities: Villa Primavera is known for its beautiful garden where guests can enjoy a leisurely stroll or relax with a book. The ambiance is tranquil and inviting.

Directions

Hotel Grand:

Address: Njegoševa 1, Cetinje, Montenegro

Getting There:

By Air: If you're flying into Montenegro, the nearest major airport is Podgorica Airport (TGD). From there, you can take a taxi or rent a car to Cetinje (approximately a 30-minute drive).

By Bus: Podgorica has a central bus station with connections to Cetinje. The bus ride takes about 45 minutes. From the Cetinje bus station, Hotel Grand is a short walk away.

Hotel Monte Rosa:

Address: Trg Ivana Crnojevića 1, Cetinje, Montenegro

Getting There:

By Air: Follow the same directions as above, from Podgorica Airport to Cetinje. Once in Cetinje, Hotel Monte Rosa is located in the central square.

By Bus: Take a bus to Cetinje and get off at the town center. Hotel Monte Rosa is conveniently located on the main square.

Hotel Ivanov Konak:

Address: Njegoševa 27, Cetinje, Montenegro

Getting There:

By Air: Arrive at Podgorica Airport and proceed to Cetinje as described earlier. Once in Cetinje, Hotel Ivanov Konak is within walking distance from the town center.

By Bus: Take a bus to Cetinje and alight in the town center. Hotel Ivanov Konak is situated close to key landmarks.

Villa Primavera:

Address: Lovćenska 8, Cetinje, Montenegro

Getting There:

By Air: Arrive at Podgorica Airport and proceed to Cetinje. Villa Primavera is located in a serene part of town. You can reach it by taxi or rental car.

By Bus: Take a bus to Cetinje and then arrange local transportation to Villa Primavera, which is situated in a peaceful residential area.

WHAT TO EAT

Konoba Kod Pera na Bukovicu:

Type: Traditional Montenegrin

Address: Bukovica bb, Cetinje

Description: Konoba Kod Pera na Bukovicu is a hidden gem known for its authentic Montenegrin cuisine. The restaurant is set in a picturesque location, offering a rustic and welcoming atmosphere. Guests can expect dishes such as slow-cooked stews, grilled meats, and locally sourced cheeses. The menu showcases the rich flavors and culinary traditions of Montenegro.

Restoran Kole:

Type: Mediterranean and Montenegrin

Address: Trg Republike, Cetinje

Description: Restoran Kole is a popular dining spot situated in the heart of Cetinje. It offers a diverse menu that combines Mediterranean and Montenegrin influences. Guests can savor a range of dishes, including fresh seafood, hearty meats, and flavorful salads. The restaurant's vibrant ambiance and central location make it a favored choice for both locals and visitors.

Kafana Dvor:

Type: Traditional Montenegrin

Address: Trg Nikole I, Cetinje

Description: Kafana Dvor is a quintessential Montenegrin tavern known for its warm hospitality and traditional cuisine. The menu features an array of dishes that highlight the robust flavors of Montenegro. From succulent grilled lamb to hearty stews and mouthwatering pastries, guests can indulge in authentic local fare. The charming setting and welcoming staff add to the overall dining experience.

Restoran Stara Varoš:

Type: Mediterranean and Montenegrin

Address: Njegoševa 6, Cetinje

Description: Restoran Stara Varoš offers a delightful fusion of Mediterranean and Montenegrin flavors. The menu boasts a diverse selection of dishes, ranging from delectable seafood creations to savory grilled meats. Guests can enjoy their meals in a cozy and inviting environment, complete with warm hospitality and a charming ambiance.

Bella Napoli:

Type: Italian

Address: Trg Nikole I, Cetinje

Description: Bella Napoli is a go-to destination for lovers of Italian cuisine. The restaurant specializes in a variety of pizzas, pastas, and Italian specialties. Guests can savor freshly prepared dishes in a comfortable and inviting setting. The menu caters to a wide range of tastes, making it a popular choice for families and individuals alike.

Kafana Galija:

Type: Traditional Montenegrin

Address: Trg Andrijevića bb, Cetinje

Description: Kafana Galija is a traditional Montenegrin tavern known for its authentic local dishes. The menu includes a selection of grilled meats, hearty stews, and delectable desserts. Guests can enjoy their meals in a cozy and convivial atmosphere, immersing themselves in the flavors of Montenegro.

Kafana Crnogorski Dvor:

Type: Traditional Montenegrin

Address: Njegoševa 36, Cetinje

Description: Kafana Crnogorski Dvor exudes a warm and inviting ambiance, making it an ideal spot for experiencing traditional Montenegrin cuisine. The menu features a variety of dishes, including succulent grilled meats, fresh fish preparations, and regional specialties. Guests can expect a memorable dining experience steeped in Montenegrin culinary traditions.

Pizzeria Oliva:

Type: Pizza and Italian

Address: Njegoševa 7, Cetinje

Description: Pizzeria Oliva is a popular choice for those craving Italian flavors, particularly pizza and pasta. The menu offers a range of pizza options with various toppings, as well as a selection of pasta dishes. Guests can enjoy their meals in a casual and comfortable setting, making it a great option for a relaxed dining experience.

WHAT TO BRING HOME

Local Handicrafts and Artwork:

Cetinje has a rich tradition of craftsmanship, with artisans creating beautiful pottery, textiles, and woodwork. Pottery may include intricately designed plates, bowls, and vases, often featuring traditional patterns and motifs. Textiles can range from embroidered linens to woven rugs, showcasing the skill and creativity of local artisans. Woodwork might include carved items like sculptures, furniture, or decorative pieces, each telling a story through their craftsmanship.

Local Food and Beverages:

Montenegro is known for its high-quality olive oil, often produced in small, family-owned olive groves. The region's wines have gained recognition for their unique flavors, especially those made from local grape varieties. Rakija, a fruit brandy, is a staple in Montenegrin culture and comes in various fruit flavors. Cheeses, such as brinza and kajmak, are also popular local products, offering a taste of Montenegrin dairy traditions.

Traditional Montenegrin Clothing:

Traditional Montenegrin clothing is rich in history and symbolism. Consider items like folk-style shirts, which often feature intricate embroidery and can be worn as a meaningful memento of your visit. Scarves, known as "marame," are also a popular accessory, and they come in various patterns and colors, each with its own significance.

Local Honey and Herbal Products:

Montenegro's diverse landscape and rich flora contribute to the production of high-quality honey. From wildflower honey to chestnut honey, you can find a range of options, each with its own distinct flavor profile. Additionally, herbal products like teas, essential oils, and skincare items are often made from locally sourced herbs and plants, offering a natural and soothing reminder of your time in Cetinje.

PLAV

Plav, nestled in the northeastern corner of Montenegro, is a town of captivating natural beauty and rich cultural heritage. It lies within the Prokletije mountain range, offering breathtaking vistas of rugged peaks and crystal-clear lakes. The town is a gateway to the spectacular Prokletije National Park, a haven for outdoor enthusiasts and nature lovers. Plav is also known for its diverse ethnic composition, with a population consisting of Montenegrins, Albanians, and Bosniaks, creating a vibrant tapestry of cultures and traditions.

The heart of Plav is the tranquil Lake Plav, surrounded by lush greenery and mirrored by the towering mountains. The lake, often compared to a fjord due to its narrow shape and steep cliffs, provides a serene setting for boating, fishing, and picnicking. Nearby, the dazzling springs of Ali Pasha and Oko Skakavice offer refreshing spots to cool off during the warm summer months.

Cultural heritage thrives in Plav, evident in its historic landmarks and religious sites. The Old Town, with its cobbled streets and Ottoman-era architecture, whispers tales of bygone eras. The elegant Redžepagić Mosque, dating back to the 17th century, stands as a testament to the town's Islamic heritage, while the Church of St. George reflects the Christian presence in Plav.

The culinary scene in Plav is a delightful fusion of Montenegrin, Albanian, and Bosniak flavors. Restaurants and eateries offer a diverse menu, featuring dishes such as sac (meat and vegetables cooked under a metal lid), delicious pies like burek, and local dairy products like kajmak and homemade cheeses. Don't miss out on sampling the region's renowned lamb dishes, cooked to perfection using traditional methods.

 Plav is an ideal destination for adventure seekers and hikers, with an abundance of trails winding through the Prokletije Mountains. The renowned "Peaks of the Balkans" trail, which traverses Montenegro, Albania, and Kosovo, starts or ends in Plav, attracting trekkers from around the world.

The town's warm and welcoming locals add to the charm of Plav, offering genuine hospitality to visitors. Markets and shops in the town center provide an opportunity to purchase local handicrafts, such as intricately woven rugs and handmade pottery.

In summary, Plav is a hidden gem in Montenegro, offering a unique blend of natural splendor, cultural diversity, and outdoor adventure.

WHAT TO DO

Explore Prokletije National Park:

Prokletije National Park is a natural wonderland, offering a diverse range of landscapes including alpine meadows, dense forests, and rugged peaks. It's a haven for hikers, mountaineers, and nature enthusiasts. You can embark on trails that lead to pristine lakes, hidden valleys, and even the highest peaks in Montenegro. Keep an eye out for unique flora and fauna, including rare species that thrive in this protected environment.

Boating and Fishing on Lake Plav:

Lake Plav is a true gem, nestled amid the Prokletije Mountains. Renting a boat or joining a guided tour allows you to fully appreciate the serenity and natural beauty that surrounds you. Fishing is a popular activity here, especially for those looking to catch trout. The calm waters and scenic backdrop create an idyllic setting for a day on the lake.

Visit Ali Pasha Springs:

Ali Pasha Springs is a natural wonder that showcases the remarkable hydrology of the region. Clear, cold water gushes forth from a limestone cave, creating a small pool below. It's not only a refreshing stop, but also a picturesque location for photographs. The lush greenery and tranquil ambiance make it a peaceful spot to unwind.

Hike to Oko Skakavice Waterfall:

This hike is a delightful adventure through the forests surrounding Plav. The path leads you to the Oko Skakavice Waterfall, a hidden gem with a striking cascade. Surrounded by lush greenery and the soothing sound of rushing water, it's a perfect spot for nature lovers and photography enthusiasts. The journey itself offers a scenic exploration of the local flora and fauna.

WHERE TO STAY

Hotel Plavski Gusar:

Location: Ulica Nikole Đokovića, Plav, Montenegro

Description: Hotel Plavski Gusar is a cozy and welcoming hotel located in the heart of Plav. The rooms are comfortably furnished, providing a relaxing environment for guests. The hotel also offers modern amenities, including free Wi-Fi, a restaurant, and a bar. Its central location makes it convenient for exploring the town and its surroundings.

Ethno Village Montenegro:

Location: Bastasi, Plav, Montenegro

Description: This charming ethno village offers a unique experience for guests looking to immerse themselves in Montenegrin village life. The wooden cottages are beautifully designed with traditional elements and equipped with modern facilities. Surrounded by stunning mountain scenery, guests can enjoy the tranquility of the natural surroundings.

Apartments Lake Views:

Location: Ulica Nikole Đokovića, Plav, Montenegro

Description: These self-catering apartments provide a comfortable and convenient accommodation option in Plav. Each apartment is well-equipped with a kitchenette, allowing guests to prepare their own meals. The highlight of these apartments is undoubtedly the stunning views of Lake Plav. The property is also within walking distance of the town center.

Guesthouse Gushan:

Location: Ulica Nikole Đokovića, Plav, Montenegro

Description: This family-run guesthouse offers a warm and inviting atmosphere for guests. The rooms are clean, comfortable, and decorated with a touch of traditional charm. The friendly hosts go out of their way to make guests feel at home. It's an ideal choice for travelers seeking a peaceful and authentic experience in Plav.

Eco Katun Vrelo:

Location: Vrelo, Plav, Montenegro

Description: For a truly unique experience, Eco Katun Vrelo offers the opportunity to stay in eco-friendly mountain huts. Nestled in a remote and picturesque area, guests can disconnect from the hustle and bustle of modern life and immerse themselves in nature. The huts are simple yet comfortable, providing a cozy retreat in the mountains.

Guesthouse Colović:

Location: Plav, Montenegro

Description: This family-operated guesthouse exudes a homely atmosphere. The rooms are clean, well-maintained, and decorated with a personal touch. Guests can expect warm hospitality from the hosts, creating a comfortable and welcoming environment.

Villa Planinska Kuća:

Location: Bastasi, Plav, Montenegro

Description: Villa Planinska Kuća offers a peaceful escape in the mountains. The villa provides stunning panoramic views of the surrounding peaks and valleys. It's an ideal choice for nature lovers and outdoor enthusiasts looking for a tranquil retreat.

Hotel Rosi:

Location: Ulica Riječka, Plav, Montenegro

Description: Hotel Rosi is a budget-friendly option that offers comfortable accommodations in the heart of Plav. The rooms are clean and well-appointed, providing a pleasant stay for guests. The hotel's central location makes it convenient for accessing the town's amenities and exploring the region.

WHAT TO EAT

Restoran Plavski Dvor:

Location: In the heart of Plav, near the central area.

Description: Restoran Plavski Dvor is a charming eatery nestled in the heart of Plav. The warm and welcoming ambiance is complemented by its rustic décor, creating a cozy atmosphere for diners. The menu is a celebration of traditional Montenegrin cuisine, featuring dishes like Ćevapi (grilled minced meat), hearty stews, and fresh fish sourced from Lake Plav. The flavors are authentic and reflect the rich culinary heritage of the region.

Restoran Belvedere:

Location: Perched on a hillside overlooking Lake Plav.

Description: Offering one of the most picturesque views in Plav, Restoran Belvedere is perched on a hillside overlooking Lake Plav. The restaurant's terrace provides a breathtaking backdrop for diners to enjoy a meal. The menu showcases a blend of Balkan and Mediterranean flavors, with a focus on grilled meats and a selection of local cheeses. The ambiance is relaxed, making it an ideal spot to unwind and savor the natural beauty of the surroundings.

Kafana Centar:

Location: Central Plav, likely near the town center.

Description: Kafana Centar is a lively gathering place for both locals and visitors alike. Its vibrant atmosphere makes it a popular spot to enjoy a diverse menu that spans from classic Balkan dishes to international fare. The outdoor seating area is particularly inviting, allowing guests to soak in the lively energy of Plav. Whether you're in the mood for a traditional stew or a global-inspired dish, Kafana Centar has something to satisfy every palate.

Picerija Braca:

Location: Central Plav near the town center.

Description: Picerija Braca is the go-to destination for pizza enthusiasts in Plav. The pizzeria prides itself on crafting delectable pies with a variety of toppings to suit all tastes. From classic Margherita to locally-inspired creations, the menu offers a wide range of options. The cozy interior and friendly service make it an excellent choice for a casual meal with friends or family.

Ribnjak Plav:

Location: Near the shores of Lake Plav.

Description: Situated near the shores of Lake Plav, Ribnjak Plav is a haven for seafood lovers. The restaurant specializes in preparing fresh fish sourced directly from the lake, ensuring a delectable dining experience. Diners can expect a menu featuring a variety of fish dishes, prepared with a blend of local herbs and spices. The serene setting adds to the overall charm, making it an idyllic spot to enjoy a leisurely meal.

Restoran Kuč:

Location: Slightly outside the town center.

Description: Restoran Kuč offers a tranquil dining experience just a short distance from Plav's town center. The restaurant is known for its peaceful ambiance and traditional Montenegrin cuisine. The menu showcases a range of dishes that highlight the authentic flavors of the region. From slow-cooked stews to grilled meats, each dish is prepared with care and attention to detail.

WHAT TO BRING HOME

Local Honey:

Details: Montenegro is renowned for its diverse flora, which contributes to the rich and varied flavors of its honey. In Plav, beekeepers often take advantage of the pristine natural surroundings, resulting in honey that is not only delicious but also carries the unique essence of the region. You can find different types of honey, from wildflower to chestnut, each with its own distinct taste profile and potential health benefits.

Handwoven Carpets and Textiles:

Details: Plav has a longstanding tradition of weaving, with skilled artisans creating intricate patterns and designs. These handwoven carpets and textiles are not only functional but also serve as exquisite pieces of art. The patterns often draw inspiration from the natural surroundings, featuring motifs like mountain landscapes, local flora, and traditional geometric shapes. Bringing home one of these pieces allows you to own a part of Plav's cultural heritage.

Cheeses and Dairy Products:

Details: Montenegrin cheeses are a culinary delight. The mountainous terrain and lush pastures provide an ideal environment for dairy farming. Some varieties, like the well-known Njeguški sir, are aged in specific conditions that result in a distinctive flavor and texture. Additionally, fresh dairy products like kajmak (a type of clotted cream) and homemade yoghurts offer a taste of authentic Montenegrin dairy craftsmanship.

Local Spirits and Wines:

Details: Plav is situated in a region with favorable conditions for viticulture. The vineyards benefit from the fertile soil and a climate that's influenced by the proximity to Lake Plav and the surrounding mountains. This creates an environment conducive to producing high-quality grapes, which are then transformed into wines with unique terroir-driven characteristics. Additionally, local spirits like rakija (fruit brandy) might be infused with regional fruits and herbs, offering a truly distinctive taste.

THE BEST FOOD IN MONTENEGRO

Njeguški pršut (Njeguši Prosciutto):

History: *Njeguški pršut*, hailed as a Montenegrin delicacy, traces its origins to the rustic village of **Njeguši** nestled amidst Montenegro's rugged mountains. This culinary tradition has endured for centuries, its inception influenced by the challenging topography of the region. In days of old, Montenegrin highlanders relied on preserving meat, a necessity dictated by the need for sustenance in the harsh mountain environment. The process of air-drying ham emerged as a practical solution, giving rise to this revered local specialty.

Directions: To experience the true essence of ***Njeguški pršut***, venture to the picturesque village of ***Njeguši***, perched in the hills overlooking the breathtaking expanse of **Kotor** Bay. Here, a myriad of eateries, ranging from humble family-owned establishments to quaint local restaurants, offer this exquisite cured ham. The air in ***Njeguši*** carries with it the essence of tradition, infusing each slice of ***pršut*** with the authentic flavors of Montenegro's culinary heritage.

Čevapi:

History: ***Čevapi***, those succulent grilled minced meat sausages, are not only a staple of Montenegrin cuisine but a testament to the country's vibrant historical tapestry. These delectable morsels are believed to have made their way into Montenegro during the epoch of Ottoman rule. Over time, they have evolved into an integral part of the local culinary landscape, celebrated for their simplicity and robust flavors.

Directions: ***Čevapi*** enthusiasts are in for a treat as they journey through Montenegro. From bustling restaurants and unassuming grills to lively street food stalls, these delectable sausages can be found across the country. For an authentic experience steeped in history, seek out eateries nestled within the ancient walls of cities like **Kotor** and **Budva**, where ***Čevapi*** are prepared with a touch of tradition and a dash of modern flair.

Buzara:

History: ***Buzara***, the flavorful seafood stew enriched with white wine, garlic, and parsley, holds a special place in Montenegro's culinary heritage. Its roots delve deep into the coastal fishing communities that have thrived along Montenegro's

Adriatic shores for centuries. In times past, when fresh catch was abundant, the preparation of **Buzara** emerged as a cherished method of showcasing the bounties of the sea.

Directions: Along the sun-kissed Adriatic coast, from the enchanting towns of **Budva** and **Kotor** to the coastal gem of **Herceg** Novi, a multitude of seafood restaurants beckon with steaming pots of exquisite **Buzara**. Each establishment adds its own touch, but the essence remains the same—a celebration of Montenegro's maritime legacy, infused with the fragrant notes of garlic and parsley.

Plješkavica:

***History:** **Plješkavica**,* a grilled meat patty that has become a beloved Balkan dish, carries echoes of the past Ottoman influence. During the era of Ottoman rule, the kebab found its way into the culinary repertoire of Montenegro, eventually evolving into the hearty, succulent *plješkavica*. This culinary transformation bears witness to the interplay of cultural exchange and local adaptation.

Directions: Across Montenegro, *plješkavica* can be savored in a variety of settings. From bustling restaurants to unassuming grills, this delectable meat patty graces menus throughout the country.

For an experience steeped in authenticity, seek out traditional taverns or local grill houses, where the art of crafting *pljeskavica* is passed down through generations.

Kačamak:

History: *Kačamak*, a robust dish crafted from a harmonious blend of cornmeal, potatoes, and cheese, finds its roots in the rugged terrain of Montenegro's northern highlands. For generations, it has stood as a cornerstone of the Montenegrin highlander's diet, a testament to the resourcefulness born of living amidst challenging mountain landscapes.

Directions: To savor the comforting embrace of *kačamak*, venture to the northern reaches of Montenegro, particularly in locales like *Žablja*k and the *Durmitor* National Park area. Here, within the warm embrace of rustic restaurants and traditional eateries, you'll encounter this hearty dish prepared with care, offering a taste of both Montenegro's natural bounty and its enduring culinary heritage. The journey to these highland regions is rewarded not only with a flavorful meal but also with breathtaking vistas of Montenegro's pristine landscapes.

FESTIVAL AND EVENT

History Enthusiasts:

Kotor Carnival (Kotor, February):

Expanded: The Kotor Carnival is a mesmerizing journey back in time, commemorating the liberation of Kotor from Venetian rule. Dating back centuries, this event sees locals and visitors alike donning elaborate masks and period costumes, transforming the streets of Kotor's Old Town into a living tableau of historical events. The air is charged with excitement as the procession winds its way through the cobbled streets, reenacting the triumphant moments of Kotor's liberation. Enthusiastic participants are encouraged to join the festivities by wearing their own costumes and becoming part of this immersive historical experience.

Perast Fasinada (Perast, July 22):

Expanded: The Perast Fasinada is a poignant maritime procession that pays tribute to an event steeped in Perast's seafaring history. On this day, the town's inhabitants don traditional attire, harking back to an era when Venetian ships patrolled these waters. As the sun sets, a solemn procession makes its way to the edge of the bay, where locals cast stones into the sea, symbolizing the sinking of a Venetian ship and commemorating the bravery of Perast's maritime community. Visitors are not only invited to observe this evocative ritual but are also welcomed to participate, adding their presence to this stirring testament to Perast's seafaring legacy.

Nature and Outdoor Enthusiasts:

Montenegro Wild Beauty Festival (Durmitor, July):

Expanded: Nestled in the heart of Durmitor National Park, the Montenegro Wild Beauty Festival is a celebration of the country's breathtaking natural landscapes. Against the backdrop of rugged mountains and pristine lakes, participants engage in a vibrant array of outdoor activities. From invigorating hikes and challenging mountaineering expeditions to exhilarating rafting adventures, the festival invites nature enthusiasts to immerse themselves in Montenegro's untamed wilderness. Cultural performances further enrich the experience, providing a glimpse into the intertwined history and heritage of this extraordinary land.

Nikšić Cultural Summer (Nikšić, July-August):

Expanded: The Nikšić Cultural Summer is a dynamic amalgamation of cultural and outdoor pursuits, making it an ideal destination for those with a diverse range of interests. Concerts resonate with melodious harmonies, theater performances captivate audiences, and exhibitions showcase the artistic tapestry of the region. For those seeking more active engagement, sporting events provide ample opportunity to partake in the spirited energy of the festival. With a kaleidoscope of offerings, visitors can tailor their experience to suit their individual passions and curiosities.

Music and Arts Lovers:

Sea Dance Festival (Budva, August):

Expanded: The Sea Dance Festival stands as a resounding testament to Montenegro's vibrant music scene. Held against the stunning backdrop of the Adriatic, this festival brings together an eclectic mix of international and local artists, gracing multiple stages with their diverse musical stylings. From pulsating beats to soulful melodies, the Sea Dance Festival promises an immersive auditory experience. Enthusiastic attendees can secure tickets to revel in the dynamic performances, becoming part of a community united by their love for music.

Kotor Art Festival (Kotor, July-August):

Expanded: The Kotor Art Festival is a veritable feast for the senses, offering a multi-dimensional experience of the arts. Within the ancient walls of Kotor, this festival unfolds in historic venues, creating a unique ambiance that enhances each performance. Classical music fills the air, theatrical productions transport audiences, visual arts captivate the eye, and cinematic creations inspire reflection. Attendees can select from a diverse array of performances and exhibitions, each contributing to the rich tapestry of cultural expression.

Culinary Enthusiasts:

Days of Fish (Herceg Novi, September):

Expanded: Days of Fish is a culinary celebration that pays homage to Montenegro's coastal cuisine, with a particular focus on the bounty of the sea. Throughout the festival, Herceg Novi transforms into a gastronomic haven, where visitors can indulge in a delectable array of fish dishes prepared by skilled local chefs. For those seeking a hands-on experience, cooking demonstrations offer insights into the artistry behind these sumptuous creations.

Wine Festivals (Various Locations, Various Dates):

Expanded: Montenegro's wine festivals serve as a delightful testament to the country's viticultural heritage. Spread across regions like Podgorica, Bar, and the Bay of Kotor, these festivals offer a sensory journey through Montenegro's vineyards and cellars. Attendees have the privilege of sampling a diverse selection of local wines, each with its unique terroir and character. Traditional food pairings complement the tasting experience, while cultural performances provide a captivating backdrop. Visitors can secure tickets for wine tastings, ensuring a memorable exploration of Montenegro's vinicultural traditions.

Religious and Cultural Observances:

Orthodox Christmas (January 7):

Expanded: Montenegro's predominantly Orthodox Christian population observes Christmas on January 7 according to the Julian calendar. This sacred occasion is marked by solemn church services, where the faithful come together to commemorate the birth of Christ. Visitors are welcomed to join in these deeply spiritual celebrations, experiencing the reverence and joy that permeates the atmosphere.

Eid al-Fitr (Varies, based on the Islamic lunar calendar):

Expanded: Eid al-Fitr, the festive culmination of Ramadan, holds a significant place in Montenegro's cultural mosaic. The towns of Podgorica and Ulcinj, with their substantial Muslim communities, come alive with the spirit of communal prayers and joyous gatherings. Visitors are warmly invited to partake in these heartfelt observances, offering a unique opportunity to share in the rich cultural heritage of Montenegro's Muslim population.

NIGHTLIFE DELIGHTS

History Enthusiasts:

Unique Nightlife Option: Old Towns' Evening Strolls

Description: Embark on a captivating journey through time with an evening stroll along the cobbled streets of Montenegro's meticulously preserved historic Old Towns. In Kotor, Budva, and Herceg Novi, centuries-old architecture tells tales of conquests, trade, and cultural exchange, providing a vivid window into the region's rich and storied past.

Best Time: The ideal period for this activity spans from spring to early autumn, when the weather is mild and conducive to leisurely exploration. However, the evenings pulse with a special vibrancy during the height of the tourist season from June to August, when these towns come alive with activity.

How to Enjoy It: Immerse yourself in the atmospheric embrace of bygone eras by wandering through narrow, winding alleys, where echoes of ancient footsteps seem to reverberate. Discover hidden squares adorned with centuries-old monuments, and step inside weathered churches that bear witness to generations of worship. Many towns offer guided evening tours led by knowledgeable locals, providing valuable historical context and captivating anecdotes that breathe life into the cobblestones.

Nature and Outdoor Enthusiasts:

Unique Nightlife Option: Beach Bars and Clubs

Description: Experience an electrifying fusion of nightlife and nature at Montenegro's beachfront bars and clubs. Nestled along the coast, these venues offer a panoramic backdrop of the shimmering Adriatic Sea. The collision of lively beats, crashing waves, and starlit skies creates an ambiance unlike any other.

Best Time: Late spring through early autumn sets the stage for beach nightlife, with July and August standing out as the zenith of vivacity. During these months, warm evenings and a bustling atmosphere converge, offering an idyllic setting for coastal revelry.

How to Enjoy It: Join beach parties that pulse to the rhythms of international DJs, or stake out a spot on the sand and dance under the stars to the backdrop of the sea's rhythmic melody. Feel the sea breeze caress your skin as you lose yourself in the euphoria of the moment. Mogren Beach in Budva and Copacabana Beach in Ulcinj are iconic destinations known for their vibrant beach nightlife.

Music and Arts Lovers:

Unique Nightlife Option: Open-Air Concerts and Music Festivals

Description: Montenegro transforms into a stage for an array of open-air concerts and music festivals, where melodies mingle with the symphony of nature. Against the backdrop of breathtaking natural vistas, these events span a spectrum of musical genres, from classical symphonies to cutting-edge contemporary beats.

Best Time: The summer months, particularly July and August, herald a crescendo of outdoor musical experiences. During this period, the country resonates with the harmonies of both local and international artists, creating an electrifying atmosphere.

How to Enjoy It: Secure tickets to your preferred event and surrender to the magic of the music. The Budva City Theater, nestled within the ancient city walls, transforms into an ethereal concert venue.

Lovćen National Park offers a stage surrounded by rugged peaks, while Porto Montenegro in Tivat provides a sophisticated backdrop for music enthusiasts.

Culinary Enthusiasts:

Unique Nightlife Option: Gourmet Dining and Wine Tasting

Description: As the sun sets, Montenegro's culinary landscape comes alive with the aroma of delectable dishes and the allure of exquisite wines. Gourmet restaurants and wine bars beckon with a gastronomic odyssey, inviting you to sample local delicacies paired with Montenegrin wines of unparalleled quality.

Best Time: While this indulgence is available year-round, the summer months are particularly enchanting. Many establishments offer outdoor seating, allowing you to dine beneath the star-studded Montenegrin sky. It's advisable to make reservations, especially during the peak tourist season.

How to Enjoy It: Make a reservation at a renowned restaurant, where expert chefs craft dishes that celebrate the region's culinary heritage. Engage in wine tasting sessions at local wineries or upscale wine bars in cities like Podgorica and Kotor. Let your taste buds embark on a journey through Montenegro's flavors, accompanied by world-class wines that complement each dish.

10 AMAZING ITINERARIES IN MONTENEGRO

Adventurous Explorer's Dream (May - September):

Activities:

- Rafting on the Tara River: Experience one of the deepest canyons in Europe while navigating thrilling rapids.
- Hiking in Durmitor National Park: Explore a UNESCO-listed park with stunning glacial lakes, rugged peaks, and diverse flora and fauna.
- Zip-lining in Durmitor: Get an adrenaline rush as you soar across breathtaking landscapes.
- Exploring the Bay of Kotor by kayak: Discover hidden coves, ancient villages, and historic sites along the stunning coast.
- Highlights: Late spring to early autumn is perfect as the weather is warm and conducive to outdoor activities. Ensure to book

adventure activities in advance to secure your spots and have a seamless experience.

Cultural Enthusiast's Delight (April - October):

Activities:

- Visit the Ostrog Monastery: A marvel of Orthodox Christianity, built into a vertical cliff face.
- Explore Kotor's Old Town: Wander through narrow, cobbled streets lined with medieval architecture and visit historical sites.
- Guided tour of Cetinje: Immerse yourself in Montenegro's royal history and visit the former capital.
- Visit the Njegos Mausoleum: Enjoy panoramic views and pay respects to a revered Montenegrin leader.
- Highlights: Spring and autumn offer mild weather, making it ideal for exploring cultural and historical sites. To avoid crowds at Ostrog Monastery, plan an early morning visit.

Beach Lover's Paradise (June - September):
Activities:

- Relax on the beaches of Budva: Enjoy the golden sands, crystal-clear waters, and vibrant nightlife.
- Explore Sveti Stefan: Marvel at the picturesque island-turned-luxury-resort.
- Boat trip around the Adriatic coast: Discover hidden coves and secluded beaches.
- Highlights: Summer is the prime time for this itinerary. For a more tranquil experience, visit the beaches during early mornings or late afternoons to avoid the midday rush.

Foodie's Journey (Year-round):
Activities:

- Taste local specialties: Savor Njeguški pršut, a famous smoked ham, indulge in fresh seafood in Kotor, and sample wines from local vineyards.
- Highlights: This itinerary can be enjoyed throughout the year, but autumn is

exceptional for foodies due to the harvest season. The flavors are rich, and the produce is at its freshest.

Historical Enthusiast's Route (April - October):

Activities:

- Visit the ancient ruins of Stari Bar: Step back in time as you explore the remnants of a once-thriving medieval town.
- Explore the Bar Aqueduct: Witness an impressive feat of engineering from the Ottoman period.
- Visit the Maritime Museum in Kotor: Learn about Montenegro's maritime history in a captivating setting.
- Highlights: Spring and autumn provide comfortable weather for exploring historical sites without the heat of summer or the chill of winter.

Nature Lover's Retreat (June - September):

Activities:

- Visit Biogradska Gora National Park: Immerse yourself in one of Europe's last rainforests, complete with a pristine glacial lake.
- Explore Skadar Lake National Park: Discover an avian paradise, rich in biodiversity, with boat trips and birdwatching opportunities.
- Hike in Lovćen National Park: Conquer peaks for breathtaking views and visit the mausoleum of Montenegro's national hero, Petar II Petrović Njegoš.
- Highlights: Summer is the ideal season, allowing you to witness Montenegro's natural beauty at its peak with lush greenery, clear skies, and warm temperatures.

Romantic Escape (May - September):

Activities:

- Take a boat trip on Lake Skadar: Share intimate moments surrounded by serene waters, lush scenery, and abundant wildlife.
- Enjoy a sunset in Perast: Witness the Adriatic turn to gold as the sun sets behind the islands.
- Have a romantic dinner in a coastal restaurant: Savor fresh seafood and local

- delicacies while basking in a romantic atmosphere.
- Highlights: Late spring to early autumn provides warm, pleasant weather perfect for a romantic getaway, whether you're cruising on Lake Skadar or dining by the sea.

Wellness and Relaxation Retreat (Year-round):

Activities:

- Enjoy spa treatments in luxury resorts around the Bay of Kotor: Rejuvenate with world-class facilities and therapies in a breathtaking coastal setting.
- Practice yoga by the sea: Find tranquility and balance while listening to the soothing sounds of the Adriatic.
- Take leisurely walks along the promenades: Immerse yourself in the natural beauty and calm ambiance of Montenegro's coastal areas.
- Highlights: Montenegro's coastal regions offer relaxation year-round. Consider visiting during the shoulder seasons or off-peak times for a quieter, more peaceful experience.

Off-the-Beaten-Path Explorer (April - October):

Activities:

- Discover the hidden gem of Ulcinj: Explore a diverse coastal town with a mix of history, culture, and stunning beaches.
- Explore Lake Plav: Enjoy the tranquility of this high-altitude lake surrounded by mountains.
- Hike to Prokletije National Park: Venture into the "Accursed Mountains" for rugged, untouched landscapes.
- Highlights: Spring to early autumn provides the best weather for exploring these less frequented destinations, allowing you to experience Montenegro off the beaten path.

Winter Wonderland (December - March):

Activities:

- Skiing in Kolašin: Hit the slopes in a picturesque winter resort surrounded by snowy peaks.

- Enjoy winter festivities in Kotor: Experience the magic of Montenegro's coastal towns during the holiday season.
- Take a snowy hike in Durmitor National Park: Witness the stunning landscapes transformed by a blanket of snow.
- Highlights: This itinerary is best enjoyed in the winter months when Montenegro offers a completely different, enchanting experience as a snowy wonderland.

TRAVELLING PRACTICALITIES

Travel Documents:

- Passport Validity: Ensure your passport is valid for at least six months beyond your planned return date. Many countries have this requirement to allow for unforeseen delays in your travel plans.
- Visa Requirements: Research whether you need a visa to enter Montenegro. Visa requirements can vary depending on your nationality. Visit the official website of the Montenegrin embassy or consulate in your country for the most up-to-date information.

Accommodation:

Advance Booking: During peak seasons, popular tourist destinations in Montenegro can get fully booked quickly. To secure the best options and rates, it's advisable to book your accommodation in advance. This also ensures you have a place to stay upon arrival.

Transportation:

- Flights: If you plan to fly into Montenegro, it's recommended to book your flights well in advance to get the best deals. The main international airports in Montenegro are Podgorica and Tivat. Compare prices and schedules from different airlines to find the most convenient option for your itinerary.
- Car Rental: If you plan to explore beyond the major cities and want the convenience of personal transportation, consider renting a car. Make sure you have an international driver's license if required. Additionally, familiarize yourself with local traffic rules and driving customs.

Local Transportation:

- Buses and Trains: Montenegro has an efficient bus system that connects cities and towns. While trains are available, they may have limited routes compared to buses. Research and plan your routes in advance, especially if you're relying on public transportation for your travels.
- Taxis and Ride-Sharing: When using taxis or ride-sharing services, always ensure that you're using licensed and reputable providers.

Ask for an estimated fare before starting your journey to avoid any surprises at the end.

Currency:

Euro (€): Montenegro uses the Euro as its official currency. While ATMs are widely available, it's recommended to carry some cash, especially for smaller establishments that may not accept credit cards.

Language:

Montenegrin: The official language in Montenegro is Montenegrin. While English is commonly spoken in tourist areas, having a few basic phrases in Montenegrin can be helpful and appreciated by locals.

Safety:

- Emergency Numbers: Familiarize yourself with the local emergency numbers for police, medical assistance, and fire services. Have them readily accessible, either saved in your phone or written down.
- Valuables: Be vigilant about your belongings, especially in crowded areas and popular tourist spots. Consider using anti-theft bags or pouches to keep your valuables secure.

Health and Safety:

- Travel Insurance: It's highly advisable to have travel insurance that covers a range of potential incidents, including medical emergencies, trip cancellations, lost luggage, and other unforeseen events. This provides you with peace of mind during your travels.
- Vaccinations: Check with your healthcare provider or a travel clinic for any recommended vaccinations or health precautions before visiting Montenegro. Make sure your routine vaccinations are up to date as well.

Local Customs and Etiquette:

- Respect for Traditions: Montenegro has a rich cultural heritage. Show respect for local customs, particularly when visiting religious sites or participating in cultural events. Dress modestly and follow any specific customs or practices that are observed.
- Dress Code: When visiting religious sites, it's appreciated to dress modestly. This usually means covering your shoulders and knees. Carry a scarf or shawl to use as a cover-up if needed.

Electrical Adapters:

Montenegro uses European-style plugs (Type C and F). If your devices use a different plug type, make sure to bring a suitable adapter to ensure you can charge your electronics.

Internet and Communication:

Consider getting a local SIM card or an international roaming plan for reliable internet access. This allows you to stay connected, use navigation apps, and communicate with locals or fellow travelers.

Time Zone:

Montenegro is in the Central European Time (CET) zone. Make sure to adjust your watch or devices accordingly to avoid any scheduling mishaps.

Local Cuisine and Dietary Needs:

If you have specific dietary requirements or allergies, communicate them to restaurants. Be aware of local dishes that may contain allergens, and don't hesitate to ask about ingredients.

Weather and Packing:

Check the weather forecast for Montenegro during your travel dates. Pack accordingly, taking into account any potential rain or cooler evenings. Don't forget essentials like sunscreen, comfortable walking shoes, and appropriate clothing for your planned activities.

CONCLUSION

In concluding our adventure through the pages of "Montenegro Travel Guide 2024 Updated," I hope you've found a treasure trove of insights and inspiration for your upcoming journey. From the charming alleys of Kotor to the wild beauty of Durmitor, this guide has aimed to be your trusty companion, offering glimpses into the heart and soul of Montenegro.

As you delve into cultural encounters, immersing yourself in the vibrant tapestry of traditions, or escape into the embrace of nature, may you find moments that etch themselves into the fabric of your memory. Let the sights, sounds, and flavors of Montenegro resonate with you long after you return.

Remember, every step you take along the Adriatic's shorelines and through the cobbled streets of ancient towns is a step into a legacy that spans centuries. Through this guide, I hope you've felt the beating heart of Montenegro, pulsing with history, culture, and breathtaking landscapes.

But above all, I want to express my deepest gratitude to you, dear reader. Thank you for entrusting me with a fragment of your journey. It's been an absolute pleasure to accompany you on this virtual adventure. May your real-life exploration of Montenegro be filled with wonder, laughter, and unforgettable moments.

Safe travels, intrepid explorer. May your path be lined with beauty, your heart be filled with warmth, and your memories be eternally sweet. Until we meet again, in the next grand adventure!

[Harrison wells]

Made in the USA
Las Vegas, NV
06 June 2024